EYEWITNESS *TRAVEL GUIDES*

LATIN AMERICAN
SPANISH
PHRASE BOOK

D1413348

A DK Publishing Book
www.dk.com

A DK PUBLISHING BOOK

www.dk.com

Compiled by Lexus Ltd with Mike Gonzalez

First American Edition, 1999
2 4 6 8 10 9 7 5 3 1

Published in the United States by DK Publishing, Inc.
95 Madison Avenue, New York, New York 10016

Library of Congress Cataloging-in-Publication Data
Latin American Spanish phrase book / by Lexus Ltd. with Mike
Gonzalez.
    p.   cm. -- (Eyewitness travel guides)
    ISBN 0–7894–4187–X (alk. paper)
    1. Spanish language--Conversation and phrase books--English.
2. Spanish language--Spoken Spanish--Latin America.
I. Gonzalez, Mike.   II. Lexus (Firm)   III. DK Publishing, Inc.
IV. Series.
PC4121.L39 1999
468.3'421--dc21   98–51187
                                                         CIP

Printed and bound in Italy by Printer Trento Srl.

CONTENTS

PREFACE

This *Eyewitness Travel Guide Phrase Book* has been compiled by experts to meet the general needs of all travelers to those South and Central American countries, Mexico, and parts of the Caribbean where Spanish is the principal language. Important characteristics of Latin American Spanish are illustrated in the Introduction, and particular variations in vocabulary and usage are indicated by abbreviated country names throughout the text. In essence, though, the language differs no more from "European" Spanish than "American" English does from "British" English.

Arranged under headings such as Hotels, Driving, and so forth, the ample selection of useful words and phrases is supported by a 2,300-line mini-dictionary. There is also an extensive menu guide listing approximately 700 dishes or methods of cooking and presentation. Typical replies to questions you may ask during your trip, and the signs or instructions you may see or hear, are shown in tinted boxes. In the main text, the pronunciation of Spanish words and phrases is imitated in English sound syllables. The Introduction gives basic guidelines to Spanish pronunciation.

The following abbreviations are used in this book for those Latin American countries where Spanish is spoken:

(*Arg*)	Argentina	(*Cos*)	Costa Rica	(*Mex*)	Mexico
(*Bol*)	Bolivia	(*Cub*)	Cuba	(*Nic*)	Nicaragua
(*CAm*)	Central	(*Ecu*)	Ecuador	(*Par*)	Paraguay
	America	(*ElS*)	El Salvador	(*Per*)	Peru
(*Chi*)	Chile	(*Gua*)	Guatemala	(*Uru*)	Uruguay
(*Col*)	Colombia	(*Hon*)	Honduras	(*Ven*)	Venezuela

Eyewitness Travel Guides are recognized as the world's best travel guides. Each title features specially commissioned color photographs, cutaways of major buildings, 3-D aerial views, and detailed maps, plus information on sights, events, hotels, restaurants, shopping, and entertainment.

PRONUNCIATION

When reading the imitated pronunciation, stress the part that is underlined. Pronounce each syllable as if it formed part of an English word and you will be understood fairly well. Remember the points below and your pronunciation will be even closer to the correct Spanish.

a	always as in "back"
g	always hard as in "get"
H	represents the guttural sound of "ch" as in the Scottish "loch"—don't pronounce this as "lock"
I	pronounced as "eye"
o	always as in "hot" (except when as *ow* below)
ow	as in "cow"
s	always sound the Spanish "s" as a double "ss" as in "missing," never like the "s" in "easy"
y	always as in "yet," not as in "why" (e.g., **siento** *syento*)

In the Spanish of Latin America, **z** and **c**, when they come before "**e**" or "**i**," are pronounced in the same way—like the English "ss" in "missing." Similarly, **v** can be spoken in such a way that it is hard to tell it apart from **b**. The English speaker should pronounce these letters like the English "v" and "b."

There are noticeable differences in the rhythm of speech between one Latin American country and another—the pronounced sing-song of Mexico, for example—but there are few differences in pronunciation between the countries. The main variations are these:

ll and **y** are pronounced "dj" (as the "g" sound in "deluge") in Argentina, Uruguay, and Paraguay, and "y" (as in "yet") elsewhere. Thus you may hear the word **llave** pronounced *djaveh* or *yaveh*.

In many Latin American countries, the final **s** of a word will not be pronounced. So for **hombres** you may hear *ombreh* rather than *ombress*.

In Mexico, Central America, and the Caribbean, the **s** is sometimes not pronounced even in the middle of a word. Thus, **piso** might be pronounced *pee-ho* rather than *peesso*.

GENDERS AND ARTICLES

Spanish has two genders for nouns—masculine and feminine. In this book, we generally give the definite article ("the")—**el** for masculine nouns, **la** for feminine nouns, **los** for masculine plural nouns, and **las** for feminine plural nouns. Where the indefinite article ("a, an") is more appropriate, we have given **un** for masculine nouns and **una** for feminine nouns or the words for "some," **unos** (masculine) and **unas** (feminine).

USE OF THE WORDS FOR "YOU" IN LATIN AMERICA

In most of Latin America, if you know people well, or they are significantly younger, you can address them with the familiar word for "you"—**tú**. However, in Argentina, Uruguay, Paraguay, and Nicaragua, a different familiar form is used—**vos**. When speaking to a stranger or to an older person you don't know well, you should always use the more formal word **Usted**. When addressing more than one person, whether you know them well or not, use the plural **Ustedes**.

BACKGROUND NOTES

Latin America was born out of a bloody encounter between cultures—the Indian culture already existing there and the Spanish seeking to conquer and colonize the continent. Other cultures came later, particularly from Africa which unwillingly supplied the slave labor to sustain the sugar plantations of the coastal lands. The variety of cultures is matched by the diversity of landscape on a land mass that embraces high mountain ranges, swamps and rain forests, deserts, and high plateaux.

This diversity is reflected in every area of culture. The dominant language is Spanish, but Portuguese, French, and English are European languages spoken by large populations. The indigenous languages spoken before the Spanish Conquest are still spoken by millions, though they have also changed and evolved. There is a great diversity of religions, sometimes working with the dominant Catholic religion, sometimes parallel to it. The range of music played, sung, and danced to across the continent is a mixture of rhythms and sounds originating in many different places, just as Latin American food is representative of tastes, methods of preparation, and ingredients from innumerable sources.

In the Andean countries of Peru, Bolivia, Colombia, and Ecuador, the mountain areas embrace many different indigenous communities, such as the Quechua and Aymará Indians. The clothes these people wear reflect a mountain life: warm capes and blankets—**ponchos** (*Per*), **ruanas** (*Ecu*)—and woolen hats—**chuyos**—to guard against the cold of the Peruvian Andes (**la sierra**) or the high Bolivian plateau (**el altiplano**). In Chile, the southern Mapuche people have begun to organize themselves politically in recent years, having suffered oppression for centuries. Mexico was home to the Aztec empire and the Maya civilization, which occupied Central America before the Spanish came. The remains of both societies are still to be seen, from the pyramids of the ancient cultures of Mexico to the rain forest city states of the Maya, which extended from Mexico to Honduras.

The small farms and village communities of the mountains are a dramatic contrast to the great modern estates (**haciendas**) of the coastal areas producing the export crops (coffee, sugar, bananas) on which many Latin American economies still depend.

By contrast Argentina and Uruguay have a strong and obvious European connection and a rather different history. The great cattle ranches and farms (**estancias**) produce the meat and wheat which Argentina exports, and the capital cities of these countries, Buenos Aires and Montevideo, are highly cosmopolitan.

Indeed, it is the cities that dominate each society, drawing the population from the countryside and presenting every aspect of contemporary Latin America. Enormous wealth, displayed in grand houses, exclusive shopping areas, and luxury hotels and restaurants, contrasts with the poverty of the shantytowns that surround every major city. Each country has its own name for the shantytowns: **pueblos jóvenes** in Peru, **callampas** in Chile, **ciudades perdidas** in Argentina, **ranchos** in Venezuela. Their inhabitants form part of the "informal" economy, many of them selling items in the streets (**los ambulantes**) or working casually. The contrast obviously produces social tensions that explode from time to time.

The Catholic Church is a presence everywhere in Latin America, having over 80 percent of the world's Catholics. Its churches, cathedrals, and monasteries are varied in style and magnificence, although they share a particularly dramatic representation of suffering in their statues and figures. Latin America has also produced the "theology of liberation," born out of the identification between religions and their local communities, and radical in its tone and activities. Other religions coexist with Catholicism, their origins in the pre-Hispanic world or the beliefs brought from Africa by slaves and kept alive in a dynamic system of worship (**santería**).

The visitor to Latin America will face a sometimes dramatic diversity and contrast. The music will change from the sentimental ballads accompanied by guitars and violins of northern Mexico (**música ranchera**) or the flamboyant trumpeters in silver studded suits of the **mariachi** to the wooden xylophones (**marimbas**) of Central America. The Andes has produced the wooden flutes (**quena**) and panpipes (**zampoña**) now so familiar elsewhere in the world. And Europe has also embraced the dance forms of Latin America, from the **tango** of Argentina to the **rumba** born of Cuban folk music and later transformed into the ubiquitous **salsa**. In Latin America, the **cumbia** is the most popular music for dancing.

SOME DOS AND DON'TS

It is hard to generalize about people's behavior across so much, and such different, social and physical terrain, but certain features do appear to be common to most Latin Americans. The most obvious is courtesy and formality when people meet. Latin Americans will generally greet those they find in a store or a bar whether they know them or not. A word and a nod of the head may be enough, but it is important that the visitor also acknowledge those he encounters.

The same is particularly true in someone's home. You will find that Latin Americans will readily invite you into their homes. When you enter a room, you should greet the people already there and shake their hand. The visitor should follow the custom and say "please" and "thank you" more often than one might in English. In part it is an excess of formality, in part a genuine acknowledgment of the other person.

Naturally enough, if you try to photograph people without asking their permission, they may well protest. Ask their permission first.

Most local people you meet will act with generosity; it seems that the poorest people are usually the most generous. If you are invited into someone's home and offered food or drink, it is rude to refuse, whether or not you feel they can afford it. It doesn't mean you have to accept everything, but it does mean that you cannot refuse unless you can find a very good excuse.

Generally, this courtesy does not extend to punctuality. Latin Americans can be infuriatingly approximate about all times and you will have to develop a strategy for dealing with everybody's casual timekeeping. Partly it is habit, but partly too that the major cities are so subject to traffic jams and crises that you simply can't tell how long any trip will take.

The other face of Latin America is officialdom, be it the endless bureaucracies or the infinite variety of uniformed personnel. They can be very oppressive, and official institutions are often very hard to penetrate. It is important not to be put off and to insist politely wherever you can. If you know you are going to cross a frontier, and you anticipate problems, dress nicely—it might help.

LOOKING AFTER YOURSELF

Diet is important. Eat well and drink lots of bottled or sterilized water—you cannot be guaranteed clean water supplies in some parts of the continent. Remember that this applies to vegetables, fruit, and fresh fruit drinks, all of which will have been washed or made with the same water. So wash the items again, and drink from bottles or cans.

Latin American food is spicy; that is its great quality. But it will affect an unaccustomed stomach. So, go prepared with some solutions for an upset stomach and assume your body will get used to the new sensations. Be prepared for the extremes of temperature: the suffocating heat of the sub-tropics (drink plenty of water and protect yourself particularly against the midday sun) and the sudden night cold of the Andes (take warm clothing with you—and sunblock for the daytime!).

USEFUL EVERYDAY PHRASES

Yes/no
Sí/No
see/no

Thank you
Gracias
grass-yass

No, thank you
No, gracias
no grass-yass

Please
Por favor
por fa-vor

I don't understand
No entiendo
no ent-yendo

Do you speak English/French/German?
¿Habla usted inglés/francés/alemán?
abla oosteh eengless/franssess/alleh-man

I can't speak Spanish
No hablo español
no ablo espan-yol

Does anyone here speak English?
¿Hay alguien que habla inglés?
I alg-yen keh abla eengless

I don't know
No sé
no seh

Please speak more slowly
Por favor, hable más lento
por fa-vor ableh mass lento

Please write it down for me
Me lo escribe por favor
meh lo eskreebeh por fa-vor

My name is . . .
Me llamo . . .
meh yamo

How do you do? *(hello)*
¿Cómo le va?
komo leh va

Very well, thank you
Muy bien, gracias
moo-ee byen grass-yass

Pleased to meet you
Mucho gusto
mootcho goosto

How are you?
¿Cómo está usted?
komo esta oosteh

Hello!/Hi!
¡Hola!
ola

Good morning
Buenos días
bweh-noss dee-ass

Good evening
Buenas tardes
bweh-nass tardess

Good night
Buenas noches
bweh-nass notchess

Good-bye/See you later
Hasta luego
asta lweh-go

Bye!
¡Chao!
chow

Excuse me! *(when sneezing, etc.)*
¡Perdón!
pairdon

(to get attention)
¡Oiga, por favor!
oyga por fa-vor

Excuse me, please *(to get past)*
Con permiso
kon pairmeesso

Sorry!
¡Disculpe!
deesskoolpeh

I'm really sorry
Le ruego me disculpe
leh roo-eh-go meh deesskoolpeh

Can you help me?
¿Me puede ayudar?
meh pweh-deh a-yoodar

Can you tell me . . .?
¿Puede decirme . . .?
pweh-deh desseermeh

13

May I have . . .?
¿Me da . . .?
meh da

I would like . . .
Quisiera . . .
keess-yaira

Is there . . . here?
¿Hay . . . aquí?
I . . . akee

Where can I get . . .?
¿Dónde consigo . . .?
dondeh konseego

How much is it?
¿Cuánto vale?
kwanto valeh

What time is it?
¿Qué hora es?
keh ora ess

What's that?
¿Qué es eso?
keh ess esso

I've lost my way
Me perdí
meh pairdee

Cheers! (*toast*)
¡Salud!
saloo

Where is the . . .?
¿Dónde está el/la . . .?
dondeh esta el/la

Where are the restrooms?
¿Dónde están los servicios/baños (Mex)?
dondeh estan loss sairveess-yoss/ban-yoss

Go away!
¡Váyase!
vaya-seh

THINGS YOU'LL HEAR

aquí tiene	here you are
¡bien!/¡bueno!	good!
¡buen viaje!	have a good trip!
¿cómo dijo?	excuse me?
¿cómo está?/¿cómo le va?	how are you?
¡cuidado!	look out!
de nada	you're welcome, don't mention it
¿de veras?	is that so?
encantado	pleased to meet you
es cierto	that's right
está bien	OK
exacto	exactly
gracias, igualmente	thank you, the same to you
¡hasta luego!	see you later!
¡hola!	hello!
¡me da mucha pena!	I'm so sorry!
muchas gracias	thank you very much
mucho gusto	nice to meet you
muy bien, gracias —¿y usted?	very well, thank you —and you?
no entiendo	I don't understand
no hay de qué	don't mention it
no sé	I don't know
¡pase!	come in!

→

15

USEFUL EVERYDAY PHRASES

por favor	please
por nada	you're welcome
¿qué dijo?	what did you say?
¿qué hay de nuevo?	what's new?
¿se puede?	may I?
sírvase usted mismo	help yourself

THINGS YOU'LL SEE

abierto	open
agua potable	drinking water
ascensor	elevator
aseos	restrooms
baños	restrooms
caballeros	men's restroom
caja	cashier
calle	street
carretera	road
cerrado (por vacaciones)	closed (for holiday period)
damas	women's restroom
día feriado/festivo	public holiday
elevador	elevator
empujar	push
entrada	way in, entrance
entrada gratis/libre	admission free
entre sin llamar	enter without knocking
feriados/festivos	public holidays
halar	pull
hombres	men's restroom
horario/horas de oficina	opening times
horario/horas de visita	visiting hours
información turística	tourist information
laborables	working days
mujeres	women's restroom
ocupado	occupied

→

peligro	danger
precaución	caution
primer piso	first floor
privado	private
prohibido	prohibited, forbidden
prohibido el paso	no trespassing
recién pintado	wet paint
reservado	reserved
salida	exit
salida de emergencia	emergency exit
se alquila departamento	apartment for rent
se arrienda departamento	apartment for rent
segundo piso	second floor
señoras	women's restroom
se prohíbe la entrada	no admittance
servicios	restrooms
se traspasa/se vende	for sale
silencio	silence, quiet
sótano	basement

DAYS, MONTHS, SEASONS

Sunday	domingo	*domeengo*
Monday	lunes	*looness*
Tuesday	martes	*martess*
Wednesday	miércoles	*myairkoless*
Thursday	jueves	*Hweh-vess*
Friday	viernes	*vyairness*
Saturday	sábado	*sabado*
January	enero	*enairo*
February	febrero	*febrairo*
March	marzo	*marsso*
April	abril	*abreel*
May	mayo	*ma-yo*
June	junio	*Hoon-yo*
July	julio	*Hool-yo*
August	agosto	*agosto*
September	septiembre	*set-yembreh*
October	octubre	*oktoobreh*
November	noviembre	*nov-yembreh*
December	diciembre	*deess-yembreh*
Spring	primavera	*preemavaira*
Summer	verano	*vairano*
Fall	otoño	*oton-yo*
Winter	invierno	*eemb-yairno*
Christmas	Navidad	*naveeda*
Christmas Eve	Nochebuena	*notcheh-bweh-na*
Easter	Pascua, Semana Santa	*paskwa, semana santa*
Good Friday	Viernes Santo	*vyairness santo*
New Year	Año Nuevo	*an-yo nweh-vo*
New Year's Eve	Nochevieja	*notcheh-vyeh-Ha*
Twelfth Night	Reyes	*ray-ess*

NUMBERS

0	cero *sairo*	10	diez *dyess*
1	uno, una* *oono, oona*	11	once *onsseh*
2	dos *doss*	12	doce *dosseh*
3	tres *tress*	13	trece *tresseh*
4	cuatro *kwatro*	14	catorce *katorsseh*
5	cinco *seenko*	15	quince *keensseh*
6	seis *sayss*	16	dieciséis *dyessee-sayss*
7	siete *see-eh-teh*	17	diecisiete *dyessee-see-eh-teh*
8	ocho *otcho*	18	dieciocho *dyessee-otcho*
9	nueve *nweh-veh*	19	diecinueve *dyessee-nweh-veh*

20 veinte *vaynteh*
21 veintiuno *vayntee-oono*
22 veintidós *vayntee-doss*
30 treinta *traynta*
31 treinta y uno *trayntı oono*
32 treinta y dos *trayntı doss*
40 cuarenta *kwarenta*
50 cincuenta *seen-kwenta*
60 sesenta *sessenta*
70 setenta *setenta*
80 ochenta *otchenta*
90 noventa *no-venta*
100 cien *syen*
110 ciento diez *syento dyess*
200 doscientos, doscientas *doss-yentoss, doss-yentass*
500 quinientos, quinientas *keen-yentoss, keen-yentass*
700 setecientos, setecientas *seh-teh-syentoss, seh-teh-syentass*
1,000 mil *meel*
1,000,000 un millón *mee-yon*

* When **uno** precedes a masculine noun, it loses the final **o**, e.g., "1 point" is **un punto**. Feminine nouns take **una**, e.g., "1 peseta" **una peseta**. With numbers in the hundreds, 200, 300, 400, etc., the form ending in **-as** is used with feminine nouns, e.g., "300 notes" **trescientos billetes**; "300 pesetas" **trescientas pesetas**.

TIME, THE CALENDAR

today	hoy	*oy*
yesterday	ayer	*a-yair*
tomorrow	mañana	*man-yana*
the day before yesterday	anteayer	*anteh-a-yair*
the day after tomorrow	pasado mañana	*passado man-yana*
this week	esta semana	*esta semana*
last week	la semana pasada	*la semana passada*
next week	la semana que viene, la semana entrante	*la semana keh vyeh-neh, la semana entranteh*
this morning	esta mañana	*esta man-yana*
this afternoon	esta tarde	*esta tardeh*
this evening		
(*up to* 7 PM)	esta tarde	*esta tardeh*
(*from* 7 PM)	esta noche	*esta notcheh*
tonight	esta noche	*esta notcheh*
yesterday afternoon	ayer por la tarde	*a-yair por la tardeh*
last night	anoche	*anotcheh*
tomorrow morning	mañana por la mañana	*man-yana por la man-ya-na*
tomorrow night	mañana por la noche	*man-yana por la notcheh*
in three days	dentro de tres días	*dentro deh tress dee-ass*
three days ago	hace tres días	*a-seh tress dee-ass*
late	tarde	*tardeh*
early	pronto	*pronto*
soon	dentro de poco	*dentro deh poko*
later on	más tarde	*mass tardeh*
at the moment	en este momento	*en esteh momento*
second	un segundo	*segoondo*
minute	un minuto	*meenooto*
two minutes	dos minutos	*doss meenootoss*

quarter of an hour	un cuarto de hora	*kwarto deh ora*
half an hour	media hora	*mehd-ya ora*
three quarters of an hour	tres cuartos de hora	*tress kwartoss deh ora*
hour	la hora	*ora*
day	el día	*dee-a*
that day	ese día	*esseh dee-a*
every day	cada día	*kada dee-a*
all day	todo el día	*todo el dee-a*
the next day	el día siguiente	*el dee-a seeg-yenteh*
week	la semana	*semana*
fortnight, 2 weeks	la quincena	*keensseh-na*
month	el mes	*mess*
year	el año	*an-yo*

TELLING TIME

The twenty-four-hour clock is commonly used in Latin America both in the written form (as in timetables) and verbally (for example, at tourist information desks, etc.). However, you will still hear the twelve-hour clock used in everyday life.

"O'clock" is not normally translated in Spanish unless it is for emphasis, when **en punto** would be used. For example: **(es) la una (en punto)** is "(it's) one o'clock," while the plural form of the verb is used for all other hours, for example: **(son) las cinco (en punto)** is "(it's) five o'clock."

The word "past" is translated by **y** "and." In order to express minutes past the hour, state the hour followed by **y** plus the number of minutes: so **las seis y diez** is "ten past six." The word "to" is translated by **para**—i.e., "there are . . . (minutes) to go before . . . ." So, for example, **veinte para las diez** means "twenty to ten." The word for "quarter" is **cuarto**; so, **un cuarto para las siete** is "quarter to seven" and **las cinco y cuarto** is "quarter past five." "Half past" is expressed using **y media**, so **las seis y media** is "half past six."

The word "at" is translated by **a** followed by **las**; for example, **a las tres y cuarto** is "at quarter past three." Remember, however, to change **las** to **la** when using "one;" thus, "at half past one" is **a la una y media**.

The expressions "AM" and "PM" have no direct equivalents but **de la mañana** "in the morning," **de la tarde** "in the afternoon/evening" (which extends up to about 7 PM in Latin America), and **de la noche** "at night"(from 7 PM) are used to distinguish between times that might be confusing. For example, "6 AM" is **las seis de la mañana** and "6 PM" is **las seis de la tarde**; "10 AM" is **las diez de la mañana** and "10 PM" is **las diez de la noche**.

what time is it?	¿qué hora es?,	*keh ora ess,*
	¿qué horas son?	*keh orass son*
one o'clock	la una	*la oona*
ten past one	la una y diez	*la oona ee dyess*
quarter past one	la una y cuarto	*la oona ee kwarto*
twenty past one	la una y veinte	*la oona ee vaynteh*
half past one	la una y media	*la oona ee mehd-ya*
twenty to two	veinte para las dos	*vaynteh para lass doss*
quarter to two	un cuarto para las dos	*kwarto para lass doss*
two o'clock	las dos (en punto)	*lass doss (en poonto)*
13:00	las trece horas	*lass treh-seh orass*
16:30	las dieciséis treinta	*lass dyessee-sayss traynta*
20:10	las veinte diez	*lass vaynteh dyess*
noon	mediodía	*mehd-yo dee-a*
midnight	medianoche	*mehd-ya notcheh*

THE CALENDAR

The cardinal numbers on page 19 are used to express the date in Spanish. However, sometimes the ordinal number may be used instead, but only when used to express "the first":

the first of May	el uno/el primero de mayo	*el oono/el preemehroh deh ma-yo*
the twentieth of June	el veinte de junio	*el vaynteh deh Hoon-yo*

HOTELS

There are an enormous variety of hotels and places to stay in Latin America. At the top of the scale are hotels classified by star ratings—the highest rating is five stars. At the lower end there may be little to distinguish hotels and **pensiones** (boarding houses). Boardinghouses may be called **pensión**, **residencia**, **posada**, **hospedaje**, **casa familiar**, or **casa de huespedes**. **Hosterías** and **dormitorios** are fairly basic and more like hostels with beds in shared rooms. Conditions in the different establishments vary from country to country, and it is possible that a **pensión** may prove to be cleaner and of a higher standard than an inexpensive hotel.

Throughout Latin America there are hotels where couples can rent rooms for an hour or two. Obviously, these are not appropriate for someone seeking a place to stay. Such establishments are often motels and might be called **motel**, **hotel garaje** (*Mex*), or **albergue transitorio** (*Arg*), but the visitor should check if in doubt.

It's best to check out the room before committing yourself. It is also a good idea to find out whether rooms have individual showers, and whether they have constant or only intermittent hot water. In less expensive hotels, showers may be operated by an electric switch on the shower itself; these are often not grounded and, therefore, can be dangerous. It's not advisable to use the shaver outlet in a bathroom for the same reason. Voltage varies from country to country.

USEFUL WORDS AND PHRASES

air-conditioned	con clima artificial	kon kleema artee-feess-yal
air conditioner	el aire acondicionado	ireh akondiss-yonado
balcony	el balcón	balkon
bathroom	el (cuarto de) baño	kwarto deh ban-yo
bathtub	la bañera, la tina	ban-yaira, teena
bed	la cama	kama

23

bed and breakfast	cuarto con desayuno	*kwarto kon dessa-yoono*
bill	la cuenta	*kwenta*
boarding-house	la pensión, la casa familiar	*penss-yon, la kassa famil-yar*
breakfast	el desayuno	*dessa-yoono*
dining room	el comedor	*komeh-dor*
dinner	la cena	*seh-na*
double bed	la cama doble, la cama matrimonial	*kama dobleh, kama matreemon-yal*
double room	un cuarto doble	*kwarto dobleh*
elevator	el ascensor, el elevador	*ass-sensor, elevador*
full board	pensión completa	*penss-yon kompleh-ta*
half board	media pensión	*mehd-ya penss-yon*
hotel	el hotel	*otel*
key	la llave	*yaveh*
lobby	la entrada	*ent-rada*
lounge	la sala	*sala*
lunch	la comida, el almuerzo	*komeeda, almwairso*
manager	el/la gerente	*Hairenteh*
receipt	el recibo	*reh-seebo*
reception	la recepción	*reh-seps-yon*
receptionist	el/la recepcionista	*reh-seps-yoneesta*
restroom	los servicios, el baño (Mex)	*sairveess-yoss, ban-yo*
room	la habitación, el cuarto, la pieza	*abeetass-yon, kwarto, pyeh-sa*
room service	el servicio de cuarto	*sairveess-yo deh kwarto*
shower	la ducha, la regadera (Mex)	*dootcha, reh-gadaira*
single bed	la cama individual	*kama eendeeveed-wal*
single room	un cuarto sencillo	*kwarto sensee-yo*

sink	el lavamanos, el lavabo	*lavamanoss, lavabo*
toilet	el retrete	*retreh-teh*
twin room	un cuarto con dos camas	*kwarto kon doss kamass*

Do you have any vacancies?
¿Tiene cuartos libres?
tyeh-neh kwartoss leebress

I have a reservation
Tengo reservación
tengo reh-sairvass-yon

I'd like a single room
Quisiera un cuarto sencillo
keess-yaira oon kwarto sensee-yo

I'd like a room with a balcony/bathroom
Quisiera un cuarto con balcón/baño
keess-yaira oon kwarto kon balkon/ban-yo

I'd like a room for one night/three nights
Quisiera un cuarto para una noche/para tres noches
keess-yaira oon kwarto para oona notcheh/para tress notchess

May I see the room?
¿Me permite ver el cuarto?
meh pairmeeteh vair el kwarto

Do you have hot water all the time?
¿Hay agua caliente constante?
I agwa kal-yenteh konstanteh

What is the charge per night?
¿Cuánto cobra por noche?
kwanto kobra por notcheh

I don't know yet how long I'll stay
Todavía no sé cuánto tiempo me voy a quedar
todavee-a no seh kwanto tyempo meh voy a keh-dar

When is breakfast/dinner?
¿A qué hora es el desayuno/la cena?
a keh ora ess el dessa-yoono/la seh-na

Please wake me at seven o'clock
Me puede llamar a las siete, por favor
meh pweh-deh yamar a lass syeh-teh por fa-vor

May I have breakfast in my room?
¿Pueden servirme el desayuno en mi cuarto?
pweh-den sairveermeh el dessa-yoono en mee kwarto

I'd like to have some laundry done
Quisiera utilizar el servicio de lavado
keess-yaira ooteeleessar el sairveess-yo deh lavado

I'll be back at ten o'clock
Regreso a las diez
reh-gresso a lass dyess

My room number is 205
El número de mi cuarto es el doscientos cinco
el noomairo deh mee kwarto ess el doss-yentoss seenko

I need a light bulb
Necesito una bombilla/un foco (Mex)/una lamparita (Arg)/
   un bombillo (Col)
*nessesseeto oona bombee-ya/oon foko/oona lampareeta/
   oon bombee-yo*

There is no toilet paper in the bathroom
Falta papel higiénico en el cuarto de baño
falta papel ee-Hyeneeko en el kwarto deh ban-yo

The window won't open
La ventana no abre
la ventana no seh abreh

There isn't any hot water
No hay agua caliente
no I agwa kal-yenteh

I'm leaving tomorrow
Me voy mañana
meh voy man-yana

When do I have to vacate the room?
¿A qué hora debo desocupar?
a keh ora deh-bo dessokoopar

May I have the bill, please?
¿Me da la cuenta, por favor?
meh da la kwenta por fa-vor

I'll pay by credit card
Quiero pagar con tarjeta (de crédito)
kyairo pagar kon tar-Heh-ta deh kredeeto

I'll pay cash
Voy a pagar en efectivo
voy a pagar en efekteevo

Can you get me a taxi?
¿Puede llamarme un taxi?
pwveh-deh yamarmeh oon taksee

Can you recommend another hotel?
¿Puede recomendarme otro hotel?
pweh-deh rekomendarmeh otro otel

THINGS YOU'LL SEE

acceso prohibido	staff only
alberca	swimming pool
albergue transitorio	motel
almuerzo	lunch
alojamiento	accommodations
ascensor	elevator
baño	bathroom
cama con desayuno	bed and breakfast

→

27

casa de huespuedes	boardinghouse
casa familiar	boardinghouse
cena	dinner
comedor	dining room
comida	lunch, meal
completo	no vacancies
cuarto con dos camas	twin room
cuarto de baño	bathroom
cuarto doble	double room
cuarto individual	single room
cuarto matrimonial	double room
cuarto sencillo	single room
cuenta	bill
desayuno	breakfast
descuento	discount
dormitorio	hostel
ducha	shower
empujar	push
entrada	entrance
escaleras	stairs
hospedaje	boardinghouse
hostería	hostel
hotel garaje	motel
jalar	pull
media pensión	half board
pensión	boardinghouse
pensión completa	full board
piscina	swimming pool
posada	boardinghouse
primer piso	first floor
prohibida la entrada	no admission
prohibido el paso	no entry
regadera	shower
residencia	boarding house
salida de emergencia	emergency exit
segundo piso	second floor

→

servicio	service charge
servicios	restroom
sólo para residentes	hotel patrons only
tocador	women's restroom

THINGS YOU'LL HEAR

A la orden?
May I help you?

Lo siento, está lleno
I'm sorry, we're full

El hotel está completo
We have no vacancies

No nos quedan habitaciones individuales/dobles
There are no single/double rooms left

¿Para cuántas noches?
For how many nights?

¿Va a pagar al contado o con tarjeta?
Will you be paying by cash or credit card?

Haga el favor de pagar por adelantado
Please pay in advance

Hay que desocupar antes de las doce
You must vacate the room by noon

CAMPING AND TRAILER TRAVEL

Camping is not as popular or as well organized as it is in much of Europe and North America, and there are very few official campsites in Latin America. Inexpensive accommodations are generally available everywhere and camping can be a risky enterprise. It is not advisable to camp anywhere other than on an official site. In Argentina, Uruguay, Chile, Mexico, and Guatemala, camping vacations are becoming more popular and official sites are opening up. Youth hostels, called **albergues** or **hosterías** (the names vary according to country), are also available—you can obtain further details from the **oficina de turismo** (tourist office) or the International Youth Hostel Federation (IYHF).

USEFUL WORDS AND PHRASES

blanket	la cobija, la manta, la frazada (*Mex, Chi, CAm*)	*kobee-нa, manta, frassada*
bucket	el cubo, el balde	*koobo, baldeh*
camper (*vehicle*)	la caravana, el tráiler	*karavana, trı-ler*
campfire	una fogata	*fogata*
go camping	acampar	*akampar*
campsite	un camping	*kampeen*
cooking utensils	los utensilios de cocina	*ootenseel-yoss deh kosseena*
drinking water	agua potable	*agwa potableh*
garbage	la basura	*bassoora*
ground cloth	la lona impermeable	*lona eempairmeh-ableh*
hitchhike	hacer auto-stop, pedir cola, pedir ráid (*CAm*), pedir aventón (*Mex*)	*assair owtostop, peh-deer kola, peh-deer rıd, peh-deer aventon*
rope	una cuerda	*kwairda*
saucepans	las cacerolas, las ollas (*Mex*)	*kassairolass, oy-ass*

sleeping bag	el saco de dormir	*sako deh dormeer*
tent	la carpa, la tienda de campaña (*Mex*)	*karpa, tyenda deh kampan-ya*
youth hostel	el albergue, la hostería	*albairgeh, ostairee-a*

Can I camp here?
¿Puedo acampar aquí?
pweh-do akampar akee

Can we park the camper here?
¿Podemos estacionar aquí el tráiler?
podeh-moss estass-yonar akee el trı-ler

Where is the nearest campsite?
¿Dónde está el camping más cercano?
dondeh esta el kampeen mass sairkano

What is the charge per night?
¿Cuánto cobra por noche?
kwanto kobra por notcheh

How much is it for a week?
¿Cuánto es para una semana?
kwanto ess para oona semana

I only want to stay for one night
Es para una noche sólo
ess para oona notcheh solo

Where is the kitchen?
¿Dónde está la cocina?
dondeh esta la kosseena

Can I light a fire here?
¿Puedo hacer fuego aquí?
pweh-do assair fweh-go akee

Where can I get . . .?
¿Dónde consigo . . .?
dondeh konseego

Is there any drinking water?
¿Hay agua potable?
I agwa potableh

THINGS YOU'LL SEE

agua	water
agua potable	drinking water
albergue juvenil	youth hostel
aseos	toilet and washroom
baños	toilet and washroom
camping	campsite
cocina	kitchen, stove
duchas	showers
estufa	stove
hostería	youth hostel
linterna	flashlight
no bañarse	no swimming
no se admiten perros	no dogs allowed
oficina de turismo	tourist office
para uso de . . .	for the use of . . .
precio	price
prohibido . . .	no . . .
prohibido acampar	no camping
prohibido el paso	no trespassing
prohibido prender fuego	no campfires
regadera	shower
se alquila	for rent
se alquilan sacos de dormir	sleeping bags for rent
se arrienda	for rent
se prohíbe . . .	. . . forbidden
tarifa	charges
tienda	store

DRIVING

There is a wide variation in the quality and type of roads the driver will find in Latin America. Major intercity highways (**autopistas**) are usually of a reasonable standard, although they will often be toll roads (**autopista de peaje**) and can be expensive. There will usually be an older and worse road without tolls. Secondary roads, by contrast, can vary greatly, and in some cases will be little more than dirt tracks (**caminos de tierra**).

Traveling across borders by car will often involve several bureaucratic procedures. Drivers should always carry registration documents and an international driver's license. Insurance requirements vary, but foreigners are usually required to take out insurance, although many local drivers won't be insured. It is normal for customs to stamp your passport or provide documentation of some kind—without this it may prove difficult to leave the country. In case of an accident, it is likely that the driver will be required to make an instant payment irrespective of who is at fault; however, it might be possible to recover this later through one's insurance.

The variety of terrain makes it advisable to use sturdy and, if possible, four-wheel drive vehicles for any trip that is likely to involve straying from the beaten path. Unleaded gas is hard to find outside Mexico, but diesel is generally available. Gas is dirtier than it is in the United States, so spark plugs, etc., should be more regularly checked.

Every village has its resident mechanic. In general, these people are very skilled, but the visitor should check prices before the work is done.

The foreign driver is always vulnerable to theft of the car or its parts. It is best not to leave the car unattended, not to leave anything in view that might encourage theft, and perhaps, if all else fails, to accept the offer from the inevitable crowd of small boys to "look after your car" in exchange for money.

It is a common occurrence in Latin America to be stopped at a roadblock on the highway or in a city. Visitors should carry all their documents with them and be ready to show them. If that is not enough, and the person who has stopped you seems intent on finding some offense to charge you with, it may be money that the person wants—and you may have to negotiate an "instant fine."

The rules of the road are: drive on the right, pass on the left. In the case of roads having equal status, or at unmarked intersections, traffic coming from the right has priority. In general, however, it is wise to assume that the rules will be ignored as often as not. Speed limits vary from country to country.

Fuel ratings are as follows: **normal**: regular; **super**: super; **extra**: premium; **gas-oil**: diesel; **sin plomo**: unleaded.

Parking is often restricted in urban areas, and cars will rapidly be towed away. Try to park in an official parking lot.

SOME COMMON ROAD SIGNS

aduana	customs
alto	stop
apagar luces	headlights off
atención al tren	beware of trains
autopista	highway
autopista de peaje	toll road
callejón sin salida	dead end
calle peatonal	pedestrian mall
calzada deteriorada	bad surface
calzada irregular	uneven surface
cambio de sentido	junction
carretera cortada	road closed
ceda el paso	yield
centro ciudad	town center
centro urbano	town center
cerrado por obras	road closed for repairs

→

circulación	traffic; traffic direction
circule despacio	slow
circunvalación	beltway
cruce	intersection
desviación	detour
desvío	detour
desvío provisional	temporary detour
escuela	school
estacionamiento	parking lot
final de autopista	end of highway
firme en mal estado	bad surface
hielo	ice
información turística	tourist information
no corretear	no passing
no hay arcén	no hard shoulder
no rebasar	no passing
obras	road work
¡ojo!	danger!
ojo al tren	beware of trains
paso a desnivel	underpass
paso a nivel	train crossing
paso subterráneo	underpass
peaje	toll
peatón, circule por la izquierda	pedestrians, keep to the left
peatones	pedestrians
peligro	danger
peligro deslizamientos	slippery road surface
precaución	caution
prender luces de cruce	headlights on
prohibido el paso	no trespassing
prohibido estacionarse	no parking
puesto de socorro	first aid
salida de camiones	roadwork exit
se usa grúa	cars will be towed away
vado permanente	in constant use (no parking) →

vehículos pesados	heavy vehicles
velocidad controlada por radar	radar speed check
zona de estacionamento limitado	restricted parking zone

USEFUL WORDS AND PHRASES

brake	el freno	*freh-no*
breakdown	una descompostura, una pana	*desskompost<u>oo</u>ra, p<u>a</u>na*
camper	la caravana, el tráiler	*karav<u>a</u>na, tr<u>i</u>-lair*
car	el auto, el automóvil, el carro (*Mex*)	*<u>ow</u>to, owtom<u>o</u>veel, k<u>a</u>rro*
clutch	el embrague	*embr<u>a</u>geh*
drive	manejar	*maneh-H<u>a</u>r*
driver's license	el carnet de conducir, el permiso de conducir, el brevete (*Per, Col*)	*karn<u>eh</u> deh kondooss<u>ee</u>r, pairm<u>ee</u>sso deh kondooss<u>ee</u>r, brev<u>eh</u>-teh*
engine	el motor	*mot<u>o</u>r*
exhaust	el tubo de escape, el exosto (*Arg*)	*t<u>oo</u>bo deh esk<u>a</u>peh, ekss-<u>o</u>sto*
fan belt	la correa del ventilador	*korr<u>eh</u>-a del venteelad<u>o</u>r*
garage (*repairs*) (*for gas*)	el taller, el garaje la gasolinera, el grifo (*Per*)	*ta-y<u>ai</u>r, gar<u>a</u>-Heh gassoleen<u>ai</u>ra, gr<u>ee</u>fo*
gas	la gasolina, la nafta (*Arg*), la bencina (*Chi*)	*gassol<u>ee</u>na, n<u>a</u>fta, bens<u>ee</u>na*
gas station	una gasolinera, un grifo (*Per*)	*gassoleen<u>ai</u>ra, gr<u>ee</u>fo*
gear	el cambio	*k<u>a</u>mb-yo*

gearbox	la caja de velocidades	*ka-Ha deh velosseedadess*
gears	los cambios	*kamb-yoss*
headlights	las luces de cruce	*loossess deh kroosseh*
highway	la autopista	*owtopeesta*
hood	el capó, el capote, el cofre *(Mex)*	*kapo, kapoteh, kofreh*
hose (pipe)	la manguera	*mangaira*
intersection	el cruce	*krooseh*
jack	el gato	*gato*
junction	el entronque	*entronkeh*
(highway entry)	una entrada de autopista	*entrada deh owtopeesta*
(highway exit)	una salida de autopista	*saleeda deh owtopeesta*
license plate	la matrícula, la placa *(Mex)*, la chapa *(Arg)*	*matreekoola, plaka, chapa*
mirror	el (espejo) retrovisor	*espeh-Ho retroveessor*
motorcycle	la moto (cicleta)	*motosseekleh-ta*
parking lot	el estacionamiento	*estass-yonam-yento*
road *(street)*	la calle	*ka-yeh*
(main road)	la carretera	*karrehtaira*
spare parts	los repuestos, las refacciones *(Mex)*	*reh-pwestoss, rehfaks-yoness*
spark plug	la bujía	*boo-Hee-a*
speed	la velocidad	*velosseeda*
speed limit	el límite de velocidad	*leemeeteh deh velosseeda*
speedometer	el cuentakilómetros	*kwenta-keelomeh-tross*
steering wheel	el volante, el timón *(Arg)*	*volanteh, teemon*
taillights	las luces piloto, las calaveras *(Mex)*	*loossess peeloto, kalavairass*

tire	la llanta,	*yanta,*
	la goma *(Arg, Uru)*,	*goma,*
	el caucho *(Ven)*	*kowcho*
tire lever	el calzo para rueda	*kalsso para rweda*
tow	remolcar	*reh-molkar*
traffic lights	el semáforo	*seh-maforo*
trailer	el remolque	*reh-molkeh*
truck	el camión	*kam-yon*
trunk	el maletero,	*maleh-tairo,*
	la maleta,	*maleh-ta,*
	el baúl *(Per)*,	*ba-ool,*
	la cajuela *(Mex)*	*kaнweh-la*
turn signal *(light)*	el intermitente	*eentairmeetenteh*
van	la camioneta	*kam-yoneta*
wheel	la rueda	*rweh-da*
windshield	el parabrisas	*parabreesass*
windshield wiper	el limpiaparabrisas	*leemp-ya parabreessass*

I'd like some gas/oil/water
Quisiera gasolina/aceite/agua
keess-yaira gassoleena/assay-teh/agwa

Fill her up, please!
¡Lleno, por favor!
yeh-no por fa-vor

35 liters of premium, please
Póngame treinta y cinco litros de extra
pongameh traynti seenko leetross deh extra

Would you check the tires, please?
¿Me revisa las llantas, por favor?
meh reveessa lass yantass por fa-vor

Do you do repairs?
¿Hacen reparaciones?
a-ssen reparass-yoness

Can you repair the clutch?
¿Pueden arreglarme el embrague?
pweh-den arreh-glarmeh el embrageh

How long will it take?
¿Cuánto tardarán?
kwanto tardaran

There is something wrong with the engine
Hay algo que marcha mal en el motor
I algo keh marcha mal en el motor

The engine is overheating
El motor se calienta demasiado
el motor seh kal-yenta demass-yado

I need a new tire
Necesito llanta nueva
nessesseeto yanta nweh-va

I'd like to rent a car
Quisiera alquilar un auto/un carro (Mex)
keess-yaira alkeelar oon owto/oon karro

I'd like an automatic/a manual
Quisiera un auto/un carro (Mex) automático/manual
keess-yaira oon owto/oon karro owtomateeko/manwal

Is there a mileage charge?
¿Tiene suplemento por kilómetro?
tyeh-neh sooplemento por keelometro

Where is the nearest garage? (for repairs)
¿Dónde está el taller más cercano?
dondeh esta el ta-yair mass sairkano

Where is the nearest gas station?
¿Dónde está la gasolinera más cercana/el grifo (Per) más cercano?
dondeh esta la gassoleenaira mass sairkana/el greefo mass sairkano

Where can I park?
¿Dónde puedo estacionarme?
dondeh pweh-do estass-yonarmeh

May I park here?
¿Puedo estacionarme aquí?
pweh-do estass-yonarmeh akee

How do I get to Lima?
¿Cómo se llega a Lima?
komo seh yeh-ga a leema

Is this the road to Monterrey?
¿Es éste el camino de Monterrey?
ess esteh el kameeno deh monteh-ray

THINGS YOU'LL HEAR

¿Lo quiere automático o manual?
Would you like an automatic or a manual?

Su carnet de conducir/permiso de conducir/licencia, por favor
May I see your driver's license, please?

Su carnet de chofer/licencia/brevete, por favor
May I see your driver's license, please?

Su pasaporte, por favor
Your passport, please

Usted ha cometido una infracción
You have committed an offense

DIRECTIONS YOU MAY BE GIVEN

a la derecha/izquierda	on the right/left
después de pasar el/la . . .	after the . . .
doble a la derecha	take a right
la primera a la derecha	first on the right
la segunda a la izquierda	second on the left
todo derecho	straight ahead
todo recto	straight ahead
voltee a la izquierda	take a left

THINGS YOU'LL SEE

aceite	oil
agua	water
aire	air
ángeles verdes	Mexican road assistance service
apague el motor	switch off engine
composturas	repairs
entrada	entrance
estacionamiento subterráneo	underground parking garage
estación de servicio	service station
extra	premium
garaje	garage
gas-oil	diesel
gasolina	gas
gasolinera	gas station
haga cola aquí	line up/wait here
introduzca el dinero exacto	insert exact change
lleno	full
magna sin	unleaded gas
nivel del aceite	oil level
normal	regular

→

41

nova	leaded gas
presión	air pressure
presión de las llantas	tire pressure
prohibido fumar	no smoking
recoja su ticket	take a ticket
reparación	repairs
salida	exit
sin plomo	unleaded
solo para residentes del hotel	hotel patrons only
super	super
taller (de reparaciones)	garage
(tren de) lavado automático	car wash
zona de servicios	service area

TRAVELING AROUND

AIR TRAVEL

Numerous international airlines provide services to the major cities of Latin America. Most Latin American countries have at least one national airline; many state airlines are currently being privatized or fused with existing private companies. Air travel within countries is also quite common and not necessarily expensive, since road and train access is not available in a number of areas—the cities of the Amazon region, for example.

TRAIN TRAVEL

Generally speaking, Latin American trains are inexpensive, though of varying degrees of comfort. Take note that the slow local trains are sometimes misleadingly called **expresos** or **rápidos**. Most trains are slow when compared to long-distance buses, even between major cities. The main types of trains are:

ferrobús	fast intercity train
autovagón	fast intercity train *(Per)*
servicio estrella	luxury intercity train *(Mex)*
rápido	moderately fast train, first class train *(Chi)*
expreso	slow train stopping at all stations, fast train *(Bol)*
tren de lujo	first class train
tren de pasajeros	passenger train
tren local	local train
tren mixto	mixed freight/passenger train

On some trains you may also have the option of a fixed seat (**asiento fijo**) or an adjustable/reclining seat (**asiento reclinable**).

Long-Distance Bus Travel

Buses remain the most popular form of travel. The range of services is wide, from the luxury air-conditioned coach (**pullman**) to the less expensive, less comfortable service (**ordinario** or **de segunda clase**). The quality of vehicles varies greatly from country to country. It is almost always necessary to book seats on long-distance buses.

Local Transportation

Local buses also vary from country to country, but they generally have a flat fare wherever you are going, show their destination on the front, and are invariably crowded. The larger, more modern buses may cost fractionally more. You can also travel in minibuses or large vans (usually called **micro** or **combi**) as well as, in some places, trucks or trucks with wooden seats.

   Mexico City, Santiago, Caracas, and Buenos Aires all have subways (**metro, subte** (*Arg*)), which also operate on a flat-fare system.

Taxi and Boat, Other Transportation

In most Latin American cities there are collective taxis (**colectivo/pesero**), which carry a number of passengers for a fixed fare on a fixed route. These vehicles will often be minibuses or large cars with distinctive markings. There are also individual taxis that can be hailed in the street if they show the "free" sign (**libre**). It is always wise to agree on a price before you get in, since drivers will frequently not use taxi meters. Airports and hotels often have taxis that are more expensive and usually more luxurious.

   In several countries water transportation is common, usually in the form of a ferry (**transbordadora**) or a smaller powered boat (**lancha**).

Useful Words and Phrases

adult	un adulto	*ad**oo**lto*
adults	mayores	*ma-y**o**ress*
air-conditioned	con aire acondicionado	*kon **i**reh akondiss-yon**a**do*
airport	el aeropuerto	*a-airopw**ai**rto*
airport shuttle	el autobús del aeropuerto	*owtob**oo**ss del a-airopw**ai**rto*
airport tax	la tasa aeroportuaria	*t**a**ssa a-airoportw**a**r-ya*
aisle seat	un asiento de pasillo	*ass-y**e**nto deh pass**ee**-yo*
baggage	el equipaje	*ekeep**a**-Heh*
baggage cart	un carrito para el equipaje	*karr**ee**to para el ekeep**a**-Heh*
baggage claim	la recogida de equipajes	*reko-H**ee**da deh ekeep**a**-Hess*
baggage room	la consigna	*kons**ee**gna*
boarding pass	la tarjeta de embarque	*tar-H**e**h-ta deh emb**a**rkeh*
boat	el barco, la lancha	*b**a**rko, l**a**ntcha*
buffet	la cafetería	*kafeh-tair**ee**-a*
bus	el autobús	*owtob**oo**ss*
(long-distance)	el ómnibus, la góndola (Chi)	*<u>o</u>mneeb**oo**ss, g**o**ndola*
(local)	el camión (Mex), la camioneta (Gua), el guagua (Cub), la micro (Chi), la buseta (Col, Ecu)	*kam-y**o**n, kam-yon**e**h-ta, w**a**-wa, m**ee**kro, booss**e**h-ta*
bus station	la terminal de autobuses, la central de autobuses	*tairmeen**a**l deh owtob**oo**ssess, sentr**a**l deh owtob**oo**ssess*
bus stop	la parada del autobús	*par**a**da del owtob**oo**ss*

car (*of train*)	el vagón, el coche	*vagon, kotcheh*
carry-on baggage	el equipaje de mano	*ekeepa-Heh deh mano*
check-in desk	la mesa de facturación	*meh-sa deh faktoorass-yon*
child	un niño/una niña	*neen-yo/neen-ya*
compartment	el compartimento	*komparteemento*
connection	una correspondencia	*koreh-spondenss-ya*
cruise	un crucero	*kroossairo*
customs	la aduana	*adwana*
departure lounge	la sala de pasajeros	*sala deh passa-Haiross*
docks	el muelle	*mweh-yeh*
domestic	nacional	*nass-yonal*
driver	el chofer	*chofer*
emergency exit	la salida de emergencia	*saleeda deh eh-mairHenss-ya*
entrance	la entrada	*entrada*
exit	la salida	*saleeda*
ferry	la transbordadora	*transborda-dora*
first class	primera (clase)	*preemaira klasseh*
fixed seat	un asiento fijo	*ass-yento fee-Ho*
flight	el vuelo	*vweh-lo*
flight number	el número de vuelo	*noomairo deh vweh-lo*
foreign exchange	el cambio de moneda	*kamb-yo deh moneh-da*
gate	la puerta (de embarque)	*pwairta deh embarkeh*
international	internacional	*eentairnass-yonal*
lost and found office	la oficina de objetos perdidos	*ofeesseena deh obHeh-toss pairdeedoss*
nonsmoking	no fumadores	*no foomadoress*
number five bus	el (autobús número) cinco	*owtobooss noomairo seenko*
one-way ticket	un boleto de ida, un pasaje de ida	*boleh-to deh eeda, passa-Heh deh eeda*

passport	el pasaporte	*passaporteh*
platform	la vía/plataforma	*vee-a/plataforma*
port	el puerto	*pwairto*
railroad	el ferrocarril	*ferro-karreel*
reclining seat	un asiento reclinable	*ass-yento rekleenableh*
reserved seat	un asiento reservado	*ass-yento reh-sairvado*
restaurant car	el coche-comedor	*kotcheh komeh-dor*
round trip ticket	un boleto de ida y vuelta, un pasaje de ida y vuelta	*boleh-to deh eeda ee vwelta, passa-Heh deh eeda ee vwelta*
schedule	el horario	*orar-yo*
seat	un asiento	*ass-yento*
second class	segunda (clase)	*segoonda klasseh*
sleeping car	el coche-dormitorio	*kotcheh dormeetoree-o*
smoking	fumadores	*foomadoress*
station	la estación	*estass-yon*
subway	el metro, el subte (*Arg*)	*meh-tro, soobteh*
taxi	un taxi	*taksee*
(collective)	un colectivo, un pesero	*kolekteevo, pessairo*
terminal (bus)	la terminal	*tairmeenal*
(train)	la estación terminal	*estass-yon tairmeenal*
ticket	un boleto, un pasaje	*boleh-to, passa-Heh*
ticket office	la oficina de boletos	*ofeesseena deh boleh-toss*
timetable	el horario	*orar-yo*
train	el tren	*tren*
transit system map	un plano	*plano*
underground passage	paso subterráneo	*passo soobterraneh-o*
waiting room	la sala de espera	*sala deh espaira*
window seat	un asiento de ventanilla	*ass-yento deh ventanee-ya*

AIR TRAVEL

A nonsmoking seat, please
Un asiento en la sección de no fumadores, por favor
oon ass-yento en la sekss-yon deh no fooma-doress por fa-vor

I'd like a window seat, please
Quisiera un asiento junto a la ventanilla, por favor
keess-yaira oon ass-yento Hoonto a la ventanee-ya por fa-vor

How long will the flight be delayed?
¿Cuánto tiempo va a demorar el vuelo?
kwanto tyempo va a demorar el vweh-lo

Which gate for the flight to Mexico City?
¿Cuál es la puerta de embarque para el vuelo de México?
kwal ess la pwairta deh embarkeh para el vweh-lo deh meh-Hee-ko

TRAIN, BUS, AND SUBWAY TRAVEL

When does the train/bus for Santiago leave?
¿A qué hora sale el tren/autobús para Santiago?
a keh ora saleh el tren/owtobooss para santee-ago

When does the train/bus from Guadalajara arrive?
¿A qué hora llega el tren/autobús de Guadalajara?
a keh ora yeh-ga el tren/owto-booss deh gwadala-Hara

When is the next train/bus to Lima?
¿A qué hora sale el próximo tren/autobús para Lima?
a keh ora saleh el prokseemo tren/owtobooss para leema

When is the first/last train/bus to Bogota?
¿A qué hora sale el primer/último tren/autobús para Bogotá?
a keh ora saleh el preemair/oolteemo tren/owtobooss para bogota

How much is it to Buenos Aires?
¿Cuánto es el boleto para Buenos Aires?
kwanto ess el boleh-to para bweh-noss i-ress

Do I have to pay a extra charge?
¿Hay que pagar suplemento?
I keh pagar soopleh-mento

Do I have to change trains?
¿Tengo que hacer correspondencia?
tengo keh assair korrespondenss-ya

Does the train/bus stop at Rosario?
¿Se para el tren/autobús en Rosario?
seh para el tren/owto-booss en rossaree-o

How long does it take to get to Cordoba?
¿Cuánto se tarda en llegar a Córdoba?
kwanto seh tarda en yeh-gar a kordoba

Where can I buy a ticket?
¿Dónde puedo comprar boleto/pasaje?
dondeh pweh-do komprar boleh-to/passa-Heh

A one-way ticket to San Salvador, please
Un boleto/un pasaje de ida a San Salvador, por favor
oon boleh-to/oon passa-Heh deh eeda a san salvador por fa-vor

---

THINGS YOU'LL HEAR

El próximo tren sale a las dieciocho horas
The next train leaves at 1800 hours

Haga la correspondencia en Cuzco
Change at Cuzco

Tiene que pagar suplemento
You must pay an extra charge

Ya no quedan asientos para Asunción
There are no more seats available for Asunción

49

A round trip ticket to Cali, please
Un boleto/un pasaje de ida y vuelta a Cali, por favor
oon boleh-to/oon passa-Heh deh eeda ee vwelta a kalee por fa-vor

Could you help me get a ticket?
¿Podría usted ayudarme a sacar boleto/pasaje?
podree-a oosteh a-yoodarmeh a sakar boleh-to/passa-Heh

I'd like to reserve a seat
Quisiera reservar un asiento
keess-yaira reh-sairvar oon ass-yento

Is this the right train/bus for Quito?
¿Es éste el tren/autobús para Quito?
ess esteh el tren/owto-booss para keeto

Is this the right platform for the Monterrey train?
¿El tren de Monterrey sale de esta vía?
el tren deh monteh-ray saleh deh esta vee-a

Which platform for the Granada train?
¿Qué vía para el tren de Granada?
keh vee-a para el tren deh granada

Is the train/bus late?
¿Se demoró el tren/autobús?
seh deh-moro el tren/owtobooss

Could you help me with my baggage, please?
¿Me ayuda con estas maletas, por favor?
meh a-yooda kon estass maleh-tass por fa-vor

Is this a nonsmoking compartment?
¿Está prohibido fumar aquí?
esta pro-eebeedo foomar akee

Is this seat free?
¿Está libre este asiento?
esta leebreh esteh ass-yento

This seat is taken
Este asiento está ocupado
esteh ass-yento esta okoopado

I have reserved this seat
Tengo reservado este asiento
tengo reh-sairvado esteh ass-yento

May I open/close the window?
¿Puedo abrir/cerrar la ventana?
pweh-do abreer/serrar la ventana

When do we arrive in Caracas?
¿A qué hora llegamos a Caracas?
a keh ora yeh-gamoss a karakass

What station is this?
¿Qué estación es ésta?
keh estass-yon ess esta

Do we stop at Cuzco?
¿Nos paramos en Cuzco?
noss paramoss en koossko

Would you keep an eye on my things for a moment?
¿Me vigila las cosas un momento?
meh veeнeela lass kossass oon momento

Is there a restaurant car on this train?
¿Tiene coche-comedor este tren?
tyeh-neh kotcheh komeh-dor esteh tren

Where is the nearest underground station?
¿Dónde está la estación de metro más cercana?
dondeh esta la estass-yon deh meh-tro mass sairkana

Where is there a bus stop?
¿Dónde hay una parada de bús?
dondeh I oona parada deh booss

Which buses go to Merida?
¿Qué autobuses van a Mérida?
keh owtoboossess van a maireeda

How often do the buses to Veracruz run?
¿Cada cuánto tiempo pasan los autobuses para Veracruz?
kada kwanto tyempo pasan loss owtoboossess para vairakrooss

Will you let me know when we're there?
¿Puede avisarme cuando lleguemos?
pweh-deh aveess-armeh kwando yeh-geh-moss

Do I have to get off yet?
¿Tengo que bajarme ya?
tengo keh ba-Harmeh ya

How do you get to Rosario?
¿Cómo se llega a Rosario?
komo seh yeh-ga a rossaree-o

Do you go near San Pedro?
¿Pasa usted cerca de San Pedro?
pasa oosteh sairka deh san peh-dro

Next stop, please!
¡Bajan!/¡Esquina!
ba-Han/eskeena

TAXI AND BOAT

Where can I get a taxi?
¿Dónde consigo un taxi?
dondeh konseego oon taksee

To the airport, please
Al aeropuerto, por favor
al a-airopwairto por fa-vor

Can you take me to the city center?
¿Me lleva al centro?
meh yeh-va al sentro

Can you let me out here?
Me deja aquí, por favor
meh deh-нa akee por fa-vor

How much is it to the station?
¿Cuánto cuesta ir a la estación?
kwanto kwesta eer a la estass-yon

That's too much!
¡Es demasiado!
ess deh-mass-yado

Could you wait here for me and take me back?
¿Me espera aquí para llevarme de regreso?
meh espaira akee para yeh-varmeh deh reh-gresso

Where can I get the ferry to Colón?
¿Dónde tomo la transbordadora para Colón?
dondeh tomo la transborda-dora para kolon

THINGS YOU'LL SEE

aduana	customs
alcoba	berth
a los trenes	to the trains
asientos	seats
atraso	delay
autovagón	fast intercity train
boletos	tickets, ticket office
bus-cama	sleeper bus
camarín	sleeping compartment
cambio de moneda	foreign exchange
camión	bus
carnet	book of subway tickets
central camionera	bus station
central de autobuses	bus station
climatizado	air-conditioned

→

coche-dormitorio	sleeper, sleeping car
colectivo	minibus, taxi
combi	collective taxi
consigna	baggage check
control de pasaportes	passport control
correspondencia	connection
demora	delay
domingos y feriados	Sundays and public holidays
entrada	entrance
entrada por delante/ por detrás	entry at the front/rear
equipajes	baggage check
escala	intermediate stop
estación	station
estación principal	central station
estación terrestre	bus station
excepto domingos	except Sundays
expreso	slow train stopping at all stations, (*Bol*) fast train
facturación	check-in
ferrobús	intercity fast train
ficha(s)	tokens for subway
fumadores	smokers
hacer correspondencia en . . .	change at . . .
hora local	local time
horario	timetable, schedule
laborables	weekdays
libre	vacant; for rent
llegadas	arrivals
mayores	adults
menores	children
metro	subway
multa por uso indebido	penalty for misuse
nacional	domestic
niños	children
no fumadores	nonsmokers

→

no fumar	no smoking
no hay parada en . . .	does not stop in . . .
no para en . . .	does not stop in . . .
ocupado	occupied
pague el importe exacto	no change given
parada	stop
pasajes	tickets, ticket office
pesero	collective taxi
por puesto	minibus
prensa	newsstand
primera clase	first class
prohibida la entrada	no entry
prohibido asomarse a la ventana	do not lean out of the window
prohibido el paso	no entry
prohibido fumar	no smoking
prohibido hablar con el chofer	do not speak to the driver
puerta de embarque	gate
puerto	harbor
puesto de periódicos	newsstand
pullman	luxury bus
rápido	moderately fast train, (Chi) first class train
recogida de equipajes	baggage claim
reservación de asientos	seat reservation
ruta	route
sala de espera	waiting room
salida	departure; exit
salida de emergencia	emergency exit
salidas	departures
salón	first class
segunda clase	second class
servicio estrella	luxury intercity train/bus
sólo laborables	weekdays only
suplemento	supplement (extra charge)

taquilla	ticket office
terminal	terminal
terminal de autobuses	bus station
terminal terrestre	bus station
tiquetes	tickets
tren de lujo	first class train
tren de pasajeros	passenger train
tren local	local train
tren mixto	mixed freight/passenger train
trenes de cercanías	local trains
utilice sólo sencillo	small change only
vagón	car (of train)
vía	platform, track
viaje	trip
vuelo	flight
vuelo directo	direct flight
vuelo regular	scheduled flight

THINGS YOU'LL HEAR

¿Lleva equipaje?
Do you have any baggage?

¿Fumadores o no fumadores?
Smoking or nonsmoking?

¿Asiento de ventanilla o de pasillo?
Window seat or aisle seat?

Está completo
It's full

Su boleto, por favor
Can I see your ticket, please?

Los boletos, por favor
Tickets, please

→

**Los pasajeros del vuelo tres dos cuatro, con destino a
Nueva York, están en estos momentos embarcando en
el avión**
Passengers for flight 324 for New York are requested to
proceed to embarkation

Pasen a la puerta (número) cuatro
Please go now to gate (number) four

Suban
Board (the train)

**El tren con destino a Granada saldrá de la vía número seis
dentro de diez minutos**
The train for Granada will leave from platform six in
ten minutes

**El tren de Monterrey llegará a la vía número uno dentro
de cinco minutos**
The train from Monterrey will arrive at platform one in
five minutes

**El tren con destino a Corinto lleva quince minutos
de retraso**
The train for Corinto is running fifteen minutes late

Sus boletos listos, por favor
Have your tickets ready, please

Abra sus maletas, por favor
Open your suitcases, please

RESTAURANTS

Restaurants (**restaurante**) vary greatly in quality and price, so look at the menu (**la carta**) first. But if the restaurant name includes the words **posada** or **mesón**, it is probably more expensive. Less expensive restaurants may carry other names, or indeed may not have a name at all. In Mexico the inexpensive eating places are called **cocina económica**, in Central America they are known as **fritanga** and **pupusería**, and in Costa Rica **soda**—but **café** is the general word. In Peru and Chile, Chinese food is found everywhere and is often inexpensive—**chifa** is the word for both Chinese food and Chinese restaurants. **Pizzerías** are universal, as are roast chicken restaurants (**rosticería** or **pollería**). There are fast food chains everywhere, and the **hamburguesas** that they sell will be immediately recognizable. Mexican food has become international and is best known for the variety of filled corn or wheat pancakes (**tortillas** and **tacos**) sold in **taquerías**. Eating out in Cuba can be difficult because of the chronic shortages affecting the economy; hotels will often have a fixed-price buffet or **oferta especial**.

If you are traveling on a tight budget, it is best to look for fixed price menus, which are usually less expensive. The signs will say **almuerzo**, **menú**, **comida típica**, **comida corriente** (*CAm*), or **comida corrida** (*Mex*), but if there is no sign you should ask if there is such a menu. The least expensive food is found in the markets, but it is probably wise to wait until you are used to the food before you eat there.

Breakfast may be a light meal, but in Mexico, for example, a hotel breakfast can be an enormous affair with fruit and eggs and meat dishes. Lunch, eaten between 2 and 4 PM, is usually the heaviest meal and will often be followed by a siesta. Certainly, lunch time is a period when very little happens. The evening meal, taken between 6 and 9 PM, will normally be lighter.

Tea, coffee, and cakes can be eaten in a **confitería** or **salón de té**. Alcohol is sold in a **bar**, or a **cantina** (*Mex*). In Mexico, there is also the **pulquería** where Mexicans drink flavored varieties of the thick white drink (**pulque**) distilled from the agave cactus. In Peru, a **chichería** is the place where you can buy local liquors. A **cervecería** (or a **choppería** in the south of the continent) sells beer.

USEFUL WORDS AND PHRASES

beer	una cerveza,	sairv<u>eh</u>-sa,
	un chop (*Chi*)	chop
bill	la cuenta	kw<u>e</u>nta
bottle	la botella	bot<u>ay</u>-ya
bread	el pan	pan
butter	la mantequilla	manteh-k<u>ee</u>-ya
café	una cafetería	kaffeh-tair<u>ee</u>-a
cake	un pastel,	past<u>e</u>l,
	un queque,	k<u>e</u>h-keh,
	una torta	t<u>o</u>rta
coffee	el café	kaff<u>e</u>h
(*black*)	un café solo,	kaff<u>e</u>h s<u>o</u>lo,
	un americano (*Mex*),	amaireek<u>a</u>no,
	un tinto (*Col*)	t<u>ee</u>nto
(*dash of milk*)	un cortado	kort<u>a</u>do
cup	la taza	t<u>a</u>ssa
fixed price	el menú, el almuerzo,	men<u>oo</u>, almw<u>ai</u>rsso,
menu	la comida típica,	kom<u>ee</u>da t<u>ee</u>peeka,
	la comida corriente (*CAm*),	kom<u>ee</u>da korr-y<u>e</u>nteh,
	la comida corrida (*Mex*)	kom<u>ee</u>da korr<u>ee</u>da
fork	el tenedor	teneh-d<u>o</u>r
glass (*tumbler*)	el vaso	v<u>a</u>-so
(*wine glass*)	la copa	k<u>o</u>pa
half liter	medio litro	m<u>e</u>hd-yo l<u>ee</u>tro
knife	el cuchillo	kootch<u>ee</u>-yo
liter	litro	l<u>ee</u>tro
menu	la carta	k<u>a</u>rta

milk	la leche	_letcheh_
mineral water	el agua mineral	_agwa meenairal_
(*uncarbonated*)	el agua mineral sin gas	_agwa meenairal seen gass_
(*carbonated*)	el agua mineral con gas	_agwa meenairal kon gass_
napkin	la servilleta	_sairvee-yeh-ta_
pepper	la pimienta	_peem-yenta_
plate	el plato	_plato_
receipt	un recibo	_resseebo_
restaurant	un restaurante	_restowranteh_
salt	la sal	_sal_
sandwich	un sandwich, una torta (*Mex*)	_sandweetch, torta_
spoon	la cuchara	_kootchara_
sugar	el azúcar, el dulce	_assookar, doolseh_
(*raw*)	el piloncillo	_peelonsee-yo_
table	la mesa	_meh-sa_
tea	el té	_teh_
(*bitter tea*)	el mate (*Arg*)	_mateh_
teaspoon	la cucharilla	_kootcharee-ya_
waiter	el mozo,	_mo-so,_
	el mesero (*Mex, CAm*),	_messairo,_
	el garzón (*Arg, Uru, Chi*),	_garsson,_
	el mesonero (*Ven*)	_messonairo_
waitress	la moza,	_mo-sa,_
	la mesera (*Mex, CAm*),	_messaira,_
	la garzona (*Arg, Uru, Chi*)	_garssona_
wine	el vino	_veeno_
wine list	la carta de vinos	_karta deh veenoss_

A table for one, please
Una mesa para uno, por favor
_oo_na m_eh_-sa p_a_ra _oo_no por fa-v_o_r

A table for two/three, please
Una mesa para dos/tres personas, por favor
_oo_na m_eh_-sa p_a_ra doss/tress pairs_o_nas por fa-v_o_r

Do you have a set menu?
¿Hay menú/comida corriente (CAm)/comida corrida (Mex)?
I men_oo_/kom_ee_da korr-y_e_nteh/kom_ee_da korr_ee_da

May we see the menu/wine list?
¿Nos trae la carta/la carta de vinos?
noss tr_a_-eh la k_a_rta/la k_a_rta deh v_ee_noss

What would you recommend?
¿Qué recomienda usted?
keh rekom-y_e_nda oost_eh_

I'd like . . .
Quisiera . . .
keess-y_ai_ra

Just coffee, please
Un café nada más, por favor
oon kaf_eh_ n_a_da mass por fa-v_o_r

A bottle of house red, please
Una botella de tinto de la casa, por favor
_oo_na bot_ay_-ya deh t_ee_nto deh la k_a_ssa por fa-v_o_r

Two more beers, please
Otras dos cervezas/chops (Chi), por favor
_o_-trass doss sairv_eh_-sass/chops por fa-v_o_r

Waiter!/Waitress!
¡Señor!/¡Señorita!
sen-y_o_r/sen-yor_ee_ta

I didn't order this
No pedí esto
no pedee esto

May we have some more . . .?
¿Nos trae más . . .?
noss tra-eh mass

May we have the bill, please?
¿Nos trae la cuenta, por favor?
noss tra-eh la kwenta por fa-vor

Can we pay separately?
Podemos pagar por separado
podeh-moss pagar por separado

That was a very good meal, thank you
La comida estuvo muy buena, gracias
la kommeeda estoovo mwee bweh-na grass-yass

My compliments to the chef!
¡Felicite al cocinero de mi parte!
feleesseeteh al kosseenairo deh mee parteh

THINGS YOU'LL HEAR

¡Buen provecho!
Enjoy your meal!

¿Qué quiere tomar?
What would you like to drink?

¿La comida ha sido de su gusto?
Did you enjoy your meal?

MENU GUIDE

aceitunas	olives
acelgas	chard
achicoria	chicory, endive
aguacate	avocado
agua de panela	drink made from water and sugar
agua mineral	mineral water
agua mineral con gas	carbonated mineral water
agua mineral sin gas	uncarbonated mineral water
aguardiente	a clear liquor similar to brandy or white rum
ahumados	smoked fish
ají	chili
ajiaco	stew of chicken, potatoes, vegetables, and corn on the cob
ajo	garlic
albaricoques	apricots
albóndigas	meatballs
alcachofas	artichokes
alcaparras	capers
al clima	at room temperature
almejas	clams
almendras	almonds
almuerzo	fixed price menu; lunch
al tiempo	at room temperature
alubias	beans
ananás	pineapple
anchoas	anchovies
anguila	eel
angulas	baby eels
anís	aniseed-flavored liquor
anticuchos	beef kabobs
api	thick custard-like drink made from corn and cinnamon
arenque	herring
arepa	cornmeal pancake
aromáticas	herb teas
arroz a la cubana	rice with fried eggs
arroz a la valenciana	rice with seafood
arroz con leche	rice pudding

arroz moro	rice with spiced meat *(Cub)*
arvejas	peas
asado	roasted meat
asado de tira	spareribs
atole	thick oats-based drink
atún	tuna
avellanas	hazelnuts
azúcar	sugar
bacalao a la vizcaína	cod served with ham, peppers, and garlic
bacalao al pil pil	cod served with chilis and garlic
baleada	cornmeal pancake filled with beans, cheese, and eggs
bandeja	main dish
bandeja paisa	beef, beans, eggs, rice, and vegetables
batido	milk shake
bebidas	drinks
berenjenas	eggplant
besugo al horno	baked sea bream
bife	steak
bistec de ternera	veal steak
bizcochos	ladyfingers
blanquillos	eggs
bolillo	roll (bread)
bonito al horno	baked tuna
bonito con tomate	tuna with tomato
boquerones fritos	fried anchovies
borracho	cake soaked in rum
brazo de gitano	sponge cake rolled up with jam filling
brevas	figs
broqueta de riñones	kidney kabobs
budín	cake
budín inglés	trifle
buñuelos	light fried pastries; doughnuts
burritos	small pancakes with sauce
buseca	oxtail soup with peas and beans
butifarra	spicy blood sausage
cabrito asado	roasted kid
cachelada	pork stew with tomatoes, onions, and garlic
cachito	croissant
café	coffee
café americano	black coffee *(Mex)*

café con leche	coffee with milk
café cortado	coffee with a dash of milk
café de olla	coffee made with cinammon and raw sugar
café perico	coffee with a dash of milk
café perfumado	coffee with a dash of brandy or other liquor
café solo	black coffee
café tinto	black coffee (Col)
caguama	turtle
calabacín/calabacita	zucchini
calabaza	pumpkin
calamares a la romana	squid rings in batter
calamares en su tinta	squid cooked in their ink
calamares fritos	fried squid
caldeirada	fish soup
caldereta gallega	vegetable stew
caldo de . . .	. . . soup
caldo de gallina	chicken soup
caldo de pescado	clear fish soup
caldo gallego	vegetable soup
caldo guanche	potato soup
callampas	mushrooms (Chi)
callos a la madrileña	tripe cooked with chilis
camarones	baby shrimp
camote	sweet potato
canelones	cannelloni
cangrejos de río	river crabs
caracoles	snails
caramelos	candy
caraotas	beans
carne de chancho	pork
carne de res	beef
carnes	meat, meat dishes
carnitas	barbecued pork
carro de queso	cheese board
castañas	chestnuts
cazuela	stew
cazuela de mariscos	seafood stew
cebada	drink made from fermented barley
cebolla	onion
cebollitas	scallions
cecina	corned beef

cena	dinner, evening meal
centollo	spider crab
cerezas	cherries
cerveza	beer
ceviche	marinated raw seafood cocktail
chairo	mutton and potato broth
champiñones	mushrooms
chancho	pork
chanquetes	fish similar to young herring
chauchas	green beans
chayote	vegetable similar to squash
chicha	drink made from corn, usually alcoholic
chícharos	peas
chicharrón	pork crackling
chifa	Chinese food
chile	chili pepper
chile poblano	green pepper (Mex)
chiles rellenos	stuffed peppers
chipirones	squid
chipotle	dark chili sauce
crentimoya	green heart-shaped fruit with white flesh
crentmol	hot sauce made from tomatoes, onion, and mint
chivito	steakburger (Uru)
choclo	corn, corn on the cob
chocolate santafereño	hot chocolate and cheese (Bol)
chocos	squid
cholgas	mussels
chongos	pot cheese in sweet syrup
chop	beer (Chi)
chuleta de . . .	. . . chop (cutlet)
chuletón	large chop (cutlet)
chuños	freeze-dried potatoes (Per, Bol)
chupete	lollipop
churisco	baked sausage
churrasco	roasted and broiled meats
churros	deep-fried pastry
cigalas	crayfish
cilantro	cilantro
ciruelas	plums
ciruelas pasas	prunes
clérico	wine, fruit, and fruit juice

cochinillo asado	roasted suckling pig
cocido	stew made with meat, chickpeas, or chicken
coco	coconut
cóctel de mariscos	seafood cocktail
codornices	quail
col	cabbage
cola de mono	eggnog (Chi)
colecillas de Bruselas	Brussels sprouts
coliflor	cauliflower
comal	griddle
comida	fixed price menu; evening meal
comida corrida	fixed price menu (Mex)
comida corriente	fixed price menu (CAm)
completo	hot dog
conejo	rabbit
conejo asado	roasted rabbit
congrio	conger eel
coñac	brandy
copa de helado	assorted ice cream
cordero	lamb
cordero asado	roasted lamb
cordero chilindrón	lamb stew
costillas de cerdo	pork ribs
cotufa	Jerusalem artichoke
crema catalana	crème brûlée
cremada	dessert made with eggs and butter
crema de espárragos	cream of asparagus soup
crepa	sweet pancake
criadillas	bull's testicles
criadillas de tierra	truffles
crocante	ice cream with chopped nuts
croquetas	croquettes
croquetas de pescado	fish croquettes
cuajada	milk curds
cuitlacoche	type of edible mushroom that grows on the corn plant
culantro	cilantro
curanto	combination dish of various meats, seafood, and vegetables (Chi)
cusuco	armadillo
cuy	guinea pig

damasco	apricot
dátiles	dates
desayuno	breakfast
dulce	sugar
durazno	peach
ejotes	pole beans
elote	corn, corn on the cob
embutidos	sausages
empanada	pastry filled with meat or fish
empanada santiaguesa	fish pie
empanadillas de bonito	tuna pies
empanadillas de carne	meat pies
enchilada	fried cornmeal pancake filled with meat, vegetables, or cheese in sauce
endivias	endive, chicory
ensalada	salad
ensalada de frutas	fruit salad
ensalada de pollo	chicken salad
ensalada mixta	mixed salad
ensaladilla rusa	Russian salad—cold diced potatoes and other vegetables in mayonnaise
entrecot de ternera	veal rib steak
entremeses de la casa	hors d'oeuvres, appetizers
epazote	herb tea (Mex)
escalope de ternera	veal scallop
escarola	curly endive
espada ahumado	smoked swordfish
espaguetis	spaghetti
espárragos	asparagus
espárragos con mayonesa	asparagus with mayonnaise
espinacas	spinach
espinacas a la crema	creamed spinach
espinazo de cerdo con patatas	stew of pork ribs with potatoes
estofado de . . .	. . . stew
estragón	tarragon
fabada (asturiana)	bean stew with sausage
faisán con castañas	pheasant with chestnuts
faisán estofado	stewed pheasant
fiambres	cold meats
fideos	thin pasta, noodles
filete a la parrilla	broiled beef
filete de cerdo	pork steak

filete de ternera	veal steak
flan	crème caramel
flan al ron	crème caramel with rum
flan de caramelo	crème caramel
flauta	cornmeal pancake, filled with chicken
flor de calabaza	pumpkin flower
frambuesas	raspberries
fresas	strawberries
fresas con crema	strawberries and cream
fresco	fruit juice (CAm)
fresones	strawberries
frijoles	kidney beans
frijoles refritos	refried beans
fritada	scraps of fried meat
fritos con jamón	fried eggs with ham
fruta	fruit
fruta variada	assorted fresh fruit
frutas en almíbar	fruit in syrup
frutillas	strawberries
gallina	chicken
gallina en pepitoria	chicken stewed with peppers
gallo pinto	rice and beans (CAm)
gallos	cornmeal pancakes filled with meat or chicken in sauce
gambas al ajillo	garlic shrimp
gambas a la americana	shrimp
gambas a la plancha	broiled shrimp
gambas con mayonesa	shrimp with mayonnaise
gambas en gabardina	shrimp in batter
gambas rebozadas	shrimp in batter
garbanzos	chickpeas
garbanzos a la catalana	chickpeas with sausage, boiled eggs, and pine nuts
garobo	iguana
gazpacho andaluz	cold tomato soup
gelatina	gelatin
gol	alcoholic drink made from butter, sugar, and milk (Chi)
gorditas	thick fried pancake with sauce
gratén de . . .	. . . au gratin—baked in a cream and cheese sauce
grelo	turnip

guacamole	avocado dip
guanábana	green heart-shaped fruit with white flesh
guarapo	hard liquor made from sugarcane
guayaba	guava—fruit with a green skin and sweet, pink flesh
guinda	black cherry; alcoholic drink made from black cherries
guindada/guindilla	cherry brandy
guineo	small banana
guisantes	peas
habas	fava beans
habas con jamón	fava beans with ham
habichuelas	beans
helado de chocolate	chocolate ice cream
helado de fresa	strawberry ice cream
helado de turrón	nut ice cream
helado de vainilla	vanilla ice cream
hígado	liver
hígado con cebolla	liver cooked with onion
hígado de ternera estofado	braised calves' liver
hígado estofado	braised liver
higos con miel y nueces	figs with honey and nuts
higos secos	dried figs
hongos	mushrooms
horchata (de chufas)	cold almond-flavored milk
hormigas culonas	large fried ants
huachinango	red snapper
huevo hilado	egg yolk garnish
huevos a la flamenca	fried eggs with ham and tomato
huevos a la mexicana	scrambled eggs with peppers, onions, and garlic
huevos cocidos	hard-boiled eggs
huevos con jamón	eggs with ham
huevos con panceta	eggs and bacon
huevos con papas fritas	fried eggs and French fries
huevos con picadillo	eggs with ground sausage
huevos con salchichas	eggs and sausages
huevos duros	hard-boiled eggs
huevos duros con mayonesa	boiled eggs with mayonnaise
huevos escalfados	poached eggs
huevos fritos	fried eggs
huevos fritos con chorizo	fried eggs with Spanish sausage

huevos pasados por agua	soft-boiled eggs
huevos pericos	scrambled eggs
huevos rancheros	fried eggs with hot tomato sauce
huevos rellenos	stuffed eggs
huevos revueltos	scrambled eggs
huevos revueltos con tomate	scrambled eggs with tomato
humitas	sweet corn tamales
húngaro	hot dog with spicy sausage in a white sauce
jaiba	crab
jalapeños	hot green chilis
jamón serrano	cured ham
jeta	pigs' cheeks
jícama	sweet turnip-like fruit eaten with lemon juice or chili
jitomate	tomato
judías verdes	green beans
judías verdes con jamón	green beans with ham
jugo	fruit juice
jugo de damasco	apricot juice
jugo de durazno	peach juice
jugo de lima	lime juice
jugo de limón	lemon juice
jugo de naranja	orange juice
jugo de piña	pineapple juice
jugo de tomate	tomato juice
langosta	lobster
langosta a la americana	lobster with brandy and garlic
langosta fría con mayonesa	cold lobster with mayonnaise
langosta gratinada	lobster au gratin
langostinos a la plancha	broiled jumbo shrimp
langostinos con mayonesa	jumbo shrimp with mayonnaise
laurel	bay leaves
leche frita	pudding made from milk, eggs, and semolina
leche merengada	cold milk with meringues
lechona	suckling pig
lechuga	lettuce
lengua de buey	ox tongue
lengua de cordero estofada	stewed lambs' tongue
lenguado a la parrilla	broiled sole
lenguado a la plancha	broiled sole

lenguado a la romana	sole in batter
lenguado frito	fried sole
lentejas	lentils
licores	liqueurs
licuado	milk shake
licuado de fresas	strawberry milk shake .
lima	lemon, lime
llapingachos	potato and cheese pancakes
locro	corn and meat soup
lombarda rellena	stuffed red cabbage
lombarda salteada	sautéed red cabbage
lomo	pork fillet
lomo curado	pork-loin sausage
lomo saltado	stir-fried pork with vegetables
lonchas de jamón	sliced, cured ham
longaniza	cooked spicy sausage
lubina a la marinera	sea bass in a parsley sauce
lubina al horno	baked sea bass
macarrones	macaroni
macarrones gratinados	macaroni and cheese
macedonia de fruta	fruit salad
macho	large green banana
maíz	corn
malta	dark beer
malteada	milk shake
mamey	round, apple-sized tropical fruit with light brown skin and sweet orange flesh
mandarinas	tangerines
maní/manises	peanuts
manitas de cordero	lamb shank
manos de cerdo	pigs' feet
manteca	butter *(Arg, Uru)*
mantecadas	small sponge cakes
mantequilla	butter
manzanas	apples
manzanas asadas	baked apples
manzanilla	dry sherry-type wine
maracuyá	passion fruit
mariscada	cold mixed shellfish
mariscos del día	fresh shellfish
mariscos del tiempo	seasonal shellfish

masa	dough
matambre arrollado	rolled beef stuffed with spinach, onion, carrots, and eggs
mate	bitter tea
mazápan	marzipan
medallones de anguila	eel steaks
medallones de merluza	hake steaks
media de agua	half bottle of mineral water
mejillones	mussels
mejillones a la marinera	mussels in a wine sauce
melocotón	peach
melocotones en almíbar	peaches in syrup
membrillo	quince gelatin
menestra de legumbres	vegetable stew
menú de la casa	fixed price menu
menú del día	fixed price menu
merengada	fruit juice with ice, milk, and sugar
merluza a la parrilla	broiled hake
merluza a la plancha	broiled hake
merluza a la romana	hake steaks in batter
merluza en salsa	hake in sauce
merluza en salsa verde	hake in a parsley and wine sauce
merluza fría	cold hake
merluza frita	fried hake
mermelada	jam
mermelada de ciruelas	prune jam
mermelada de damasco	apricot jam
mermelada de durazno	peach jam
mermelada de frambuesas	raspberry jam
mermelada de fresas	strawberry jam
mermelada de naranja	orange marmalade
mero	grouper (type of fish)
mero a la parrilla	broiled grouper
mero en salsa verde	grouper in garlic and parsley
mezcal	liquor distilled from the maguey cactus
milanesa	breaded chop or scallop
mole	thick dark chili sauce, or dessert made from banana and chocolate (Gua)
mollejas de ternera fritas	fried sweetbreads
mondongo	tripe
mora	blackberry

MENU GUIDE

morros de cerdo	pigs' cheeks
morros de vaca	cows' cheeks
mortadela	salami-type sausage
morteruelo	type of ground meat pie
mosh	oats with cinammon and honey (Gua)
nabo	turnip
nacatamales	cornmeal dough filled with meat in sauce and steamed in banana leaves
naranjas	oranges
natillas	cold custard
natillas de chocolate	cold custard with chocolate
níscalos	wild mushrooms
nísperos	fruit like crab apples
nixtamal	cornmeal dough
nopalitos	pickled chopped cactus leaves
nueces	walnuts
orejas de cerdo	pigs' ears
ostras	oysters
otros mariscos según precios en plaza	other shellfish, depending on prices
pabellón	ground meat, beans, rice, and banana (Ven)
pachamanca	traditional Peruvian dish of meats cooked in clay
pacumutu	beef kabobs
paella	fried rice with various meats
paella valenciana	rice with shellfish, chicken, etc.
paila	fried or poached eggs with bread
paleta de cordero lechal	shoulder of lamb
palta	avocado
pan	bread
pana	liver (Chi)
panache de verduras	vegetable stew
pan de higos	dried fig cake with cinnamon
pan dulce	buns and cakes
panceta	bacon
pancita	tripe
papa	potato
papa rellena	stuffed potato (Per)
papas a la criolla	potatoes in hot, spicy sauce

papas a la huancaína	stuffed potato (Per)
papas asadas	baked potatoes
papas bravas	potatoes in cayenne pepper
papas fritas	French fries
papaya	papaya
pargo	fish
parrillada de caza	mixed broiled game
parrillada de mariscos	mixed broiled shellfish
pasas	raisins
pastel de . . .	. . . cake
pastel de ternera	veal pie
pasteles	cakes
pasticho	lasagna (Ven)
patacón	mashed potato and banana (Col)
patatas	potato chips
patín	tomato-based sauce
patitos rellenos	stuffed duckling
pato asado	roasted duck
pato a la naranja	duck à l'orange
pato estofado	stewed duck
pavipollo	large chicken
pavo asado	roasted turkey
pavo relleno	stuffed turkey
pecho de ternera	breast of veal
pechuga de pollo	breast of chicken
pepián	meat stew
pepinillos	gherkins
pepinillos en vinagreta	gherkins in vinaigrette sauce
pepino	cucumber
peras	pears
percebes	edible barnacles
perdices	partridges
perdices asadas	roasted partridges
perdices con chocolate	partridges with chocolate
perejil	parsley
pescaditos fritos	fried fish
pestiños	sugared pastries
píbil	dark sauce
picadillo	ground meat
picadillo de ternera	ground veal
picante/picoso	hot, spicy
pichón	pigeon

piloncillo	raw sugar
pimienta	black pepper
pimientos a la riojana	baked red peppers fried in oil
pimientos fritos	fried peppers
pimientos morrones	strong peppers
pimientos rellenos	stuffed peppers
pimientos verdes	green peppers
pinchitos	snacks served in bars
pincho	kabob
pinchos morunos	kabobs
pinolillo	alcoholic drink made from toasted seeds
piña fresca	fresh pineapple
piñones	pine nuts
pipián	hot chili sauce
pique macho	chopped beef with onions
pisco	clear liquor made from grapes
pisco sour	drink made from pisco, lemon juice, and egg whites
pisto	fried mixed vegetables
pisto manchego	marrow with onion and tomato
pitahaya	red fruit of a cactus plant with soft, sweet flesh
plátanos	bananas
plátanos flameados	flambéed bananas
plato montañero	beef, sausage, beans, eggs, and rice
poblano	green pepper (Mex)
pollo al ajillo	fried chicken with garlic
pollo a la parrilla	broiled chicken
pollo al vino blanco	chicken in white wine
pollo asado	roasted chicken
pollo braseado	braised chicken
pollo con tomate	chicken with tomatoes
pollo con verduras	chicken and vegetables
pollo en cacerola	chicken casserole
pollo en pepitoria	chicken in wine with saffron, garlic, and almonds
pollo salteado	sautéed chicken
polvorones	sugar-based dessert
pomelo	grapefruit
porotos	kidney beans
postre	dessert

potaje	thick broth
potaje de garbanzos	chickpea stew
pozole	corn and meat stew
puchero canario	meat casserole with chickpeas
puerco chuk	pork stew
pulpitos con cebolla	baby octopus with onions
pulpo	octopus
pulque	thick alcoholic drink distilled from the pulp of the agave cactus (*Mex*)
pupusa	dumpling usually filled with cheese or meat (*CAm*)
puré de papas	mashed potatoes, potato purée
puro de caña	sugarcane liquor
purrusalda	cod with leeks and potatoes
queque	cake
quesadilla	fried cornmeal pancake usually filled with cheese or meat
queso	cheese
queso del país	local cheese
queso de oveja	sheep cheese
quisquillas	shrimp
rábanos	radish
ragout de ternera	veal stew
rajas	broiled green peppers
rape a la cazuela	stewed monkfish
rape a la plancha	broiled monkfish
raya	skate
redondo al horno	roasted fillet of beef
refresco	soft drink, carbonated drink
refritos	refried beans
remolacha	beets
repollo	cabbage
repostería de la casa	cakes baked on the premises
requesón	cream cheese, cottage cheese
res	beef
riñones	kidneys
riñones al jerez	kidneys with sherry
róbalo	bass
rocoto	hot red pepper
rodaballo	turbot (type of flounder)
romero	rosemary
ron	rum

ropa vieja	shredded meat
rosca	traditional sponge cake
roscas	sweet pastries
saice/saisi	spicy meat broth (Bol)
sajta	chicken in hot sauce (Bol)
sal	salt
salchichas	sausages
salchichón	white sausage with pepper
salmón ahumado	smoked salmon
salmón a la parrilla	broiled salmon
salmonetes	red mullet
salmonetes a la parrilla	broiled red mullet
salmonetes en papillote	red mullet cooked in foil
salmón frío	cold salmon
salmorejo	thick sauce made with bread
salpicón de mariscos	shellfish with vinaigrette
salsa ali oli/allioli	mayonnaise with garlic
salsa bechamel	white sauce
salsa de tomate	tomato sauce
salsa holandesa	hollandaise sauce
salsa mahonesa/mayonesa	mayonnaise
salsa tártara	tartar sauce
salsa verde	hot sauce with chili and tomatoes
salsa vinagreta	vinaigrette sauce
salteño	small pie usually filled with chicken or other meat and sauce
sancocho	vegetable soup with meat or fish
sandía	watermelon
sangría	sangría—mixture of red wine, lemon juice, sugar, and fruit
sardinas a la brasa	barbecued sardines
sardinas a la parrilla	broiled sardines
sardinas fritas	fried sardines
seco	dry; main dish
seco de . . .	. . . stew
semidulce	medium-sweet
sesos	brains
setas	mushrooms
sidra	cider
silpancho	beef with eggs (Bol)
singani	grape liquor
sobreasada	soft red sausage with cayenne

solomillo frio	cold roasted beef
solomillo con patatas	fillet steak with French fries
solomillo de ternera	fillet of veal
sopa	soup
sopa de ajo	garlic soup
sopa de almendras	almond-based pudding
sopa de fideos	noodle soup
sopa de gallina	chicken soup
sopa del día	soup of the day
sopa de lentejas	lentil soup
sopa de marisco	fish and shellfish soup
sopa de mondongo	tripe stew (Hon)
sopa de pescado	fish soup
sopa de tortilla	soup with cornmeal pancakes
sopa de verduras	vegetable soup
sopa mallorquina	soup with tomatoes and meat
sopa seca	rice course
sopa sevillana	fish and mayonnaise soup
sorbete	sorbet; ice cream (CAm); fruit juice with cream (Col)
soufflé de queso	cheese soufflé
surubí	a freshwater fish
taco	cornmeal pancake usually filled with beef or chicken
tajadas	fried banana strips
tallarines	noodles
tallarines a la italiana	tagliatelle
tamales	cornmeal dough filled with meat and sauce then steamed in banana leaves
tamarindo	tamarind
tapado	stew
tarta de almendra	rich almond cake
tarta de chocolate	rich chocolate cake
tarta de fresas	strawberry tart or cake
tarta de manzana	apple tart
tarta helada	rich ice-cream cake
tarta moca	mocha tart
tequila	alcohol distilled from the pulp of the agave cactus (Mex)
ternera asada	roasted veal
tocino	bacon

tomates rellenos	stuffed tomatoes
tomillo	thyme
tordo	thrush
toronja	grapefruit
torrejas	French toast
torrijas	sweet pastries
torta	cake, pie; filled roll (Mex)
tortilla	cornmeal pancake
tortilla de harina	wheat flour pancake
tortilla de huevo	omelette
tostadas	fried crisp pancake with sauce
trucha ahumada	smoked trout
trucha con jamón	trout with ham
truchas molinera	trout meunière—trout dipped in flour, fried, and served with butter, lemon juice, and parsley
tuna	prickly pear
tuntas	freeze-dried potatoes (Gua)
turrón	nougat
turrón de Jijona	soft nougat
uvas	grapes
vainitas	green beans
vieiras	scallops
vino blanco	white wine
vino rosado	rosé wine
vino tinto	red wine
vuelvealavida	marinated seafood cocktail with chili
yaguarlocro	potato soup with sausage
yerba mate	herbal tea
yuca	cassava
zanahorias	carrots
zapallo	squash
zapote	sweet pumpkin
zarzamoras	blackberries
zarzuela de mariscos	seafood stew

STORES AND SERVICES

This chapter covers all sorts of shopping needs and services.
To start with you'll find some general phrases that can be used
in lots of different places—many of them are named in the list
below. After the general phrases come some more specific
requests and sentences to use when you've found what you
need, whether it is food, clothing, repairs, developing film, a
haircut, or to bargain in the market. Don't forget to refer to the
mini-dictionary for items you may be looking for.

Store hours vary considerably from country to country and
region to region. In hot areas, for example, stores may often
open very early in the morning, then close until late afternoon
or early evening. In the major cities, stores will usually remain
open until 8 PM, but may close for lunch between 1 and 4 PM.
The majority of stores are closed on Sundays.

Toiletries and nonmedical items can be bought at supermarkets
and department stores; medicines are only sold in a **farmacia**.
(See Health page 110 for details about drugstores.)

A lot of shopping in Latin America will be done in markets,
where prices are variable and bargaining is common. You
should ask whether the price is fixed "**¿Es precio fijo?**"
(*ess press-yo fee-HO*), and if the answer is ambiguous, bargaining
can then begin.

USEFUL WORDS AND PHRASES

bag	una bolsa	*bolsa*
bakery	la panadería	*panadairee-a*
(*selling pastries*)	la pastelería	*pasteh-lairee-a*
bookstore	la librería	*leebrairee-a*
butcher's	la carnicería	*karneesairee-a*
buy	comprar	*komprar*
camera store	la tienda fotográfica	*tyenda fotografeeka*
camping	equipos de camping	*ekeeposs deh*
equipment		*kampeen*

STORES AND SERVICES

candy store	la dulcería,	*doolssairee-a,*
	la confitería	*konfeetairee-a*
cash register	la caja	*ka-Ha*
cashier	la caja	*ka-Ha*
craft store	la tienda de	*tyenda deh*
	artesanías	*artessanee-ass*
department	los grandes	*grandess*
store	almacenes	*almasseh-ness*
dry cleaner	la tintorería	*teentoreree-a*
electrical	la tienda de	*tyenda deh*
goods store	electrodomésticos	*elektrodomesteekoss*
expensive	caro	*ka-ro*
fish market	la pescadería	*peskadairee-a*
gift store	la tienda de regalos	*tyenda deh rega-loss*
greengrocer's	la frutería	*frooteree-a*
grocery store	el almacén, la tienda	*alma-sen, tyenda*
	de abarrotes/	*deh abar-rotes/*
	alimentos,	*aleemen-toss,*
	el boliche	*bolee-cheh,*
	(Chi, Arg, Uru),	
	la pulpería *(Cos, ElS),*	*poolpairee-a,*
	la bodega *(Gua, Nic)*	*bodeh-ga*
hairdresser's	la peluquería	*pelookairee-a*
hardware	la ferretería,	*ferreh-tairee-a,*
store	la tlapalería *(Mex)*	*tlap-alairee-a*
inexpensive	barato	*bara-to*
jewelry store	la joyería	*Hoy-airee-a*
laundromat	la lavandería	*lavanderee-a*
	automática	*owto-mateeka*
market	el mercado,	*mairkado,*
	la feria *(Arg, Uru),*	*fairee-a,*
	el tianguis *(Mex)*	*tyan-gees*
menswear	ropa de hombres	*ro-pa deh om-bress*
newsstand	el puesto de	*pweh-sto deh*
	periódicos	*pairee-odeekoss*
optician's	la óptica	*opteeka*
pastry shop	la pastelería	*pasteh-lairee-a*

receipt	el recibo	*resseebo*
record store	la discoteca	*deeskoteh-ka*
sale	rebajas,	*reba-нass,*
	liquidación,	*leekeedass-yon,*
	gangas (*Mex*)	*gan-gass*
shoe repairs	reparación de	*reparass-yon deh*
	calzado	*kalssado*
shoe store	la zapatería	*sapatairee-a*
shopping center	el centro comercial	*sentro komairss-yal*
souvenir store	la tienda de regalos	*tyenda deh rega-loss*
stationery store	la papelería	*papeh-lairee-a*
store	la tienda, el almacén	*tyenda, alma-sen*
supermarket	el supermercado	*soopermairkado*
tailor	la sastrería	*sastrairee-a*
tobacco store	la tabaquería	*tabakairee-a*
toy store	la juguetería	*нoogheh-tairee-a*
travel agency	la agencia de viajes	*aнenssee-a deh vya-нess*
womens' wear	ropa de señoras	*ro-pa deh sen-yorass*

Excuse me, where is/are . . .? (*in a supermarket*)
Disculpe, ¿dónde está/están . . .?
deesskoolpeh dondeh esta/estan

Where is there a . . . (store)?
¿Dónde hay una (tienda de) . . .?
dondeh I oona tyenda deh

Where is the . . . department?
¿Dónde está la sección de . . .?
dondeh esta la sekss-yon deh

Is there a market here?
¿Hay un mercado/una feria (*Arg, Uru*)/un tianguis (*Mex*) aquí?
I oon mairkado/oona fairee-a/oon tyan-gees akee

I'd like . . .
Quisiera . . .
keess-yaira

Do you have . . .?
¿Tienen . . .?
tyeh-nen

How much is this?
¿Cuánto vale esto?
kwanto va-leh esto

Where do I pay?
¿Dónde se paga/se cobra?
dondeh seh paga/seh ko-bra

Do you take credit cards?
¿Puedo pagar con tarjeta de crédito?
pweh-do pagar kon tarheh-ta deh kredeeto

I think perhaps you've shortchanged me
Me parece que me ha dado cambio de menos
meh pareh-seh keh meh a dado kamb-yo deh menoss

May I have a receipt?
¿Me puede dar recibo?
meh pweh-deh dar resseebo

May I have a bag, please?
¿Me da una bolsa, por favor?
meh da oona bolsa por fa-vor

I'm just looking
Sólo estoy mirando
so-lo estoy meerando

I'll come back later
Regresaré luego
reh-gressareh lweh-go

Do you have any more of these?
¿Tiene más de éstos?
tyeh-neh mass deh estoss

Do you have anything less expensive?
¿Tiene algo más barato?
tyeh-neh algo mass barato

Do you have anything larger/smaller?
¿Tiene algo más grande/pequeño?
tyeh-neh algo mass grandeh/peh-ken-yo

May I try it (them) on?
¿Puedo probármelo(s)?
pweh-do probarmeh-lo(ss)

Does it come in other colors?
¿Lo hay en otros colores?
lo I en otross koloress

It's too big/small for me
Me queda grande/pequeño
meh keh-da grandeh/peh-ken-yo

Could you gift-wrap it for me?
¿Podría envolvérmelo para regalo?
podree-a emvol-vairmeh-lo para rega-lo

I'd like to exchange this, it's damaged
Quiero que me cambien esto porque tiene un defecto
kyairo keh meh kamb-yen esto por-keh tyeh-neh oon defekto

I'm afraid I don't have the receipt
Lo lamento, no tengo el recibo
lo lamentoh, no tengo el resseebo

May I have a refund?
¿Pueden reembolsarme (el dinero)?
pweh-den reh-embolsarmeh (el deenairo)

Where can I get this repaired?
¿Dónde me pueden arreglar esto?
dondeh meh pweh-den arreh-glar esto

Can you repair this?
¿Puede repararme esto?
pweh-deh reh-pararmeh esto

I'd like this skirt/these pants dry-cleaned
Quisiera que me limpien esta falda/estos pantalones
keess-yaira keh meh leemp-yen esta falda/estoss pantalo-ness

I'd like to make an appointment
Quiero hacer una cita
kyairo assair oona seeta

I want a cut and blow-dry
Quisiera un corte y moldeado con secador de mano
keess-yaira oon korteh ee moldeh-ado kon sekador deh mano

Just a trim, please
Recórtemelo un poco solamente, por favor
rekorteh-meh-lo oon poko solamenteh por fa-vor

When does the market open?
¿A qué hora abre el mercado?
a keh ora seh a-breh el mairkado

What's the price per kilo?
¿Cuánto vale el kilo?
kwanto valeh el keelo

Is it a fixed price?
¿Es precio fijo?
ess press-yo fee-Ho

That's too much! I'll give you . . .
¡Es mucho! Le doy . . .
ess mootcho! leh doy

That's fine. I'll take it
Está bien. Me lo llevo
esta byen. meh lo yeh-vo

I'll have a piece of that cheese
Me da un pedazo de ese queso
meh da oon pedasso deh esseh keh-so

About 250/500 grams
Como doscientos cincuenta/quinientos gramos
komo doss-yentoss seen-kwenta/keen-yentoss gra-moss

A kilo/half a kilo of apples, please
Un kilo/medio kilo de manzanas, por favor
oon keelo/meh-dyo keelo deh manssanass por fa-vor

THINGS YOU'LL SEE

abarrotes	grocery store
abierto	open
agencia de viajes	travel agency
alimentos	groceries
alquiler	rental, rent
autoservicio	self-service
barato	inexpensive
bricolage	do-it-yourself supplies
caja	cash register, cashier
calidad	quality
calzados	shoe store
carnicería	butcher's
cerrado	closed
cerrado por vacaciones	closed for holidays
cerramos los . . .	closed on . . .
droguería	drugstore
ferretería	hardware store
flores	flowers
ganga	bargain
grandes almacenes	department store
hagalousted mismo	do-it-yourself
helados	ice cream

→

juguetes	toys
lavado de pelo	shampoo
librería	bookstore
liquidación total	stock clearance
moda	fashion
moldeado con secador de mano	blow-dry
mueblería/muebles	furniture store
no se admiten devoluciones	no refunds given
no tocar	do not touch
oferta	special offer
panadería	bakery
papelería	stationery store
pastelería	pastry shop
peluquería de hombres	men's hairdresser
peluquería de señoras	womens' hairdresser
planta inferior	lower floor
planta superior	upper floor
por favor, use una cesta/ un carrito	please take a basket/cart
precio	price
rebajado	reduced
rebajas	bargains
rebajas de verano	summer sale
revelado	developing
ropa de hombres	menswear
saldos	sales
salón de peluquería	hairdressing salon
sección	department
señoras	womens' department
sorbete	ice cream, fruit juice with cream (*Col*)
tabaquería	tobacco store
tintorería	dry cleaner

→

tlapalería	hardware store
ultramarinos	grocery store
venta	sale
verduras	vegetables

THINGS YOU'LL HEAR

¿Le están atendiendo?
Are you being helped?

¿Qué desea?/¿Qué se le ofrece?
May I help you?

¿No tiene suelto/sencillo?
Don't you have anything smaller? *(money)*

Lo siento, se nos han terminado
I'm sorry, we're out of stock

Esto es todo lo que tenemos
This is all we have

No podemos devolver el importe/el dinero
We cannot give cash refunds

¿Desea algo más?
Will there be anything else?

¿Cuánto quisiera?
How much would you like?

¿Le importa que sea un poco más?
Does it matter if it's a bit over?

Lo siento, no aceptamos tarjetas de crédito
I'm afraid we don't take credit cards

¿Cómo quiere que se lo corte?
How would you like it cut?

SPORTS

Soccer (**el fútbol**) dominates the Latin American sports scene, from north to south. But every other sport has its fans and its participants throughout Latin America. In Cuba and Central America, for example, baseball (**el béisbol**) is almost more important than soccer. And in Mexico, football (**el fútbol americano**) is popular, particularly among students. Every country other than landlocked Bolivia and Paraguay has its beaches or access to the water, and although newer water sports such as sailboarding are still largely restricted to the resorts frequented by foreign tourists, you'll be able to go snorkeling or underwater fishing in many places. Argentina and Uruguay have equestrian sports of every kind; polo, however, is entirely restricted to the wealthier classes. Chile's mountainous landscape has allowed the development of skiing and mountaineering. Golf, while played everywhere, is largely inaccessible to any but the better-off local people.

The Spanish legacy remains in both the wall game (**pelota** or **jai alai**) and the bullfight (**los toros**). The latter is still popular in parts of Latin America, although it is conducted in slightly different ways from Spain. In Central America the bullfights are less ritualistic and often more direct, as amateur fighters tackle the bulls.

USEFUL WORDS AND PHRASES

athletics	el atletismo	atleh-t_ee_ssmo
badminton	el badminton	b_a_dmeenton
ball	la pelota, el balón	peh-l_o_ta, bal_o_n
baseball	el béisbol	b_a_yssbol
basketball	el básquet,	b_a_ssket,
	el baloncesto	balons_e_sto
bicycle	una bicicleta	beesseekl_eh_-ta
boxing	el box	boks
bullfight	los toros	t_o_ross

canoe	una piragua,	peer_a_gwa,
	una canoa	kan_o_-a
canoeing	el piragüismo	peerag-w_ee_ssmo
car racing	las carreras de autos	kar-r_ai_rass deh _o_wtoss
cycling	el ciclismo	seekl_ee_ssmo
diving board	un trampolín	trampol_ee_n
fishing	la pesca	p_e_ska
fishing rod	una caña de pescar	k_a_n-ya deh peskar
flippers	las aletas	al_e_h-tass
football	el fútbol americano	f_oo_tbol amairee-k_a_no
goggles	las gafas de bucear	g_a_fass deh boosseh-_a_r
golf	el golf	"golf"
golf course	un campo de golf	k_a_mpo deh golf
hang gliding	el ala delta	_a_la d_e_lta
horse racing	las carreras de	kar-r_ai_rass deh
	caballos	kab_a_-yoss
hunting	la caza	k_a_ssa
mountaineering	el andinismo	andeen_ee_ssmo
oxygen bottles	las botellas de	bot_ay_-yass deh
	oxígeno	oks_ee_-нeno
pedal boat	un hidropedal	eedroped_a_l
racket	una raqueta	rak_e_h-ta
ride (horse)	montar a caballo	montar a kab_a_-yo
riding	la equitación	ekeetass-y_o_n
rock climbing	la escalada en rocas	esskal_a_da en r_o_kass
sail (noun)	la vela	v_e_h-la
(verb)	navegar (a vela)	naveg_a_r a v_e_h-la
sailboard	una tabla de	t_a_bla deh
	windsurfing	weends_oo_rfeen
sailing	vela	v_e_h-la
skin diving	el submarinismo	soobmaree-n_ee_ssmo
snorkel	el respirador	respeera-d_o_r
soccer	el fútbol sóccer	f_oo_tbol s_o_kair
soccer ball	el balón	bal_o_n
soccer game	un partido de fútbol	part_ee_do deh f_oo_tbol
sports center	el centro deportivo	s_e_ntro deport_ee_vo

stadium	el estadio	*estad-yo*
surfboard	la tabla de surfing	*tabla deh soorfeen*
swim	nadar	*nadar*
swimming pool	la alberca	*albairka*
tennis	el tenis	*teh-neess*
tennis court	una cancha de tenis	*kancha deh teh-neess*
tennis racket	una raqueta de tenis	*rakeh-ta deh teh-neess*
underwater fishing	la pesca submarina	*peska soobmareena*
volleyball	el voleibol	*volay-bol*
waterskiing	el esquí acuático	*eskee akwateeko*
water skis	los esquís acuáticos	*eskeess akwateekos*
go windsurfing	hacer windsurfing	*assair weendsoorfeen*
wrestling	la lucha libre	*lootcha leebreh*
yacht	un yate	*ya-teh*

How do I get to the beach?
¿Cómo llego a la playa?
komo yeh-go a la pla-ya

How deep is the water here?
¿Qué profundidad tiene el agua aquí?
keh profoondee-da tyeh-neh el agwa akee

Is it safe to swim here?
¿Se puede nadar sin peligro aquí?
seh pweh-deh nadar seen pelee-gro akee

Can I fish here?
¿Puedo pescar aquí?
pweh-do peskar akee

I would like to rent a bicycle
Quisiera alquilar una bicicleta
keess-yaira alkeelar oona beesseeklеh-ta

How much does it cost per hour/day?
¿Cuánto vale la hora/el día?
kwanto valeh la ora/el dee-a

I would like to take waterskiing lessons
Quisiera tomar clases de esquí acuático
keess-yaira tomar klasess deh eskee akwateeko

Where can I rent . . .?
¿Dónde puedo alquilar . . .?
dondeh pweh-do alkeelar

I haven't played this before
Nunca había jugado esto
noonka abee-a Hoogado esto

What's the score?
¿A cómo van?
a komo van

THINGS YOU'LL SEE

acceso playa	to the beach
alberca	swimming pool
alquiler de botes	boats to rent
alquiler de sombrillas	beach umbrellas to rent
alquiler de tablas	board rental
alquiler de tumbonas	deck chairs to rent
autódromo	race car track
balneario	swimming pool; resort
cancha de tenis	tennis court
corriente peligrosa	dangerous current
hipódromo	racetrack (*horses*)
peligro	danger
piscina	swimming pool
prohibido bañarse	no swimming
prohibido pescar	no fishing
socorrista	lifeguard
velódromo	bicycle track

POST OFFICES AND BANKS

Post offices in Latin America deal only with mail and telegrams, so don't look for a phone there. Use a telephone booth or find the telephone exchange (see Telephones page 99). Stamps (**estampillas**) can be bought in the post office or in some stores; for example, stationery stores and bookstores. In some post offices you can pay the postage and have the item franked (**franqueado**) instead of buying a stamp. You can also send packages from a separate counter at the post office. They should be registered (**certificado**), especially if they are being sent abroad. Sometimes packages sent outside the country need to be passed by customs (**la aduana**).

Bank opening hours vary from country to country, but normally they are open Monday to Friday from 8 or 8:30 AM to 1 or 1:30 PM, and from 2 to 4:30 PM. Nevertheless, you will need to check in each area. Foreign exchange counters (**cambios**) in banks are sometimes open only in the morning. On Saturday mornings larger banks in city centers may sometimes open, usually until 12:30 PM. Each transaction in the bank will normally be carried out at a different window, and you may often be passed from one to the other. At the exchange window, for example, you may be given a form to take to the cashier (**la caja**). Each window, of course, has its own separate line. Bear in mind that many people are paid their salaries through the bank, and, on pay day (the first of the month, for example), the banks will often be very crowded. ATMs are becoming more common, however.

USEFUL WORDS AND PHRASES

airmail	correo aéreo	*korreh-o a-aireh-o*
ATM	el cajero automático	*ka-Hairo owtomateeko*
bank	el banco	*banko*
bill (*currency*)	un billete de banco	*bee-yeh-teh deh banko*
cash	dinero	*deenairo*

change *(noun)*	sencillo, suelto	*sensee-yo, swelto*
(verb)	cambiar	*kamb-yar*
check	un check	*cheh-keh*
checkbook	el libro de checks, la checkra	*leebro deh cheh-kess, cheh-kayra*
credit card	la tarjeta de crédito	*tarHeh-ta deh kredeeto*
customs form	el impreso para la aduana	*eempreh-so para la adwana*
delivery	el reparto	*reh-parto*
deposit *(noun)*	un ingreso	*eengreh-so*
dollar *(US)*	el dólar	*dolar*
exchange rate	el tipo de cambio	*teepo deh kamb-yo*
fax *(noun)*	un fax	*faks*
(verb)	mandar por fax	*mandar por faks*
form	un impreso	*eempreh-so*
international money order	un giro internacional	*Heero eentairnass-yonal*
letter	una carta	*karta*
mail *(noun)*	el correo	*korreh-o*
(verb)	echar al buzón	*etchar al boosson*
mailbox	el buzón	*boosson*
mailman	el cartero	*kartairo*
money order	un giro (postal)	*Heero postal*
package	un paquete	*pakeh-teh*
postage rates	las tarifas postales	*tareefass postaless*
postal order	un giro postal	*Heero postal*
postcard	una postal	*postal*
poste restante	la lista de correos	*leesta deh korreh-oss*
post office	(la oficina de) Correos	*offeesseena deh korreh-oss*
pound sterling	la libra esterlina	*leebra esterleena*
registered letter	una carta certificada	*karta sairteefee-kada*
stamp	una estampilla, un timbre *(Mex)*	*estampee-ya, teembreh*
surface mail	correo terrestre	*korreh-o tair-restreh*

telegram	un telegrama	*teleh-grama*
traveler's check	un check de	*cheh-keh deh*
	viajero	*vya-Hairo*
withdrawal	una retirada	*reteerada*
zip code	la zona postal	*sona postal*

How much is a letter/postcard to America?
¿Cuánto vale la estampilla para una carta/una postal a Estados Unidos?
kwanto valeh la estampee-ya para oona karta/oona postal estadoss ooneedoss

I would like three 200 peso stamps
Quisiera tres timbres de doscientos pesos
keess-yaira tress teembress deh doss-syentoss peh-soss

I want to register this letter
Quiero mandar esta carta certificada
kyairo mandar esta karta sairteefee-kada

I want to send this package to Canada
Quiero mandar este paquete a Canadá
kyairo mandar esteh pakeh-teh a kanada

How long does the mail to America take?
¿Cuánto demora el correo para Estados Unidos?
kwanto deh-mora el korreh-o para estadoss ooneedoss

Is there any mail for me?
¿Hay correo para mí?
i korreh-o para mee

I'd like to send a telegram/a fax
Quisiera mandar un telegrama/un fax
kveess-yaira mandar oon teleh-grama/oon fax

This is to go airmail
Quiero mandar esto por correo aéreo
kyairo mandar esto por korreh-o a-aireh-o

I'd like to change this into pesos
Quisiera cambiar esto por pesos
keess-y<u>ai</u>ra kamb-y<u>a</u>r <u>e</u>sto por p<u>e</u>h-soss

Can I cash these traveler's checks?
Puedo cambiar estos checks de viajero
pw<u>e</u>h-do kamb-y<u>a</u>r <u>e</u>stoss ch<u>e</u>h-kess deh vya-H<u>ai</u>ro

Can I have it in 5,000 peso notes, please?
¿Me lo puede dar en billetes de cinco mil pesos, por favor?
*meh lo pw<u>e</u>h-deh dar en bee-y<u>e</u>h-tess deh s<u>ee</u>nko meel p<u>e</u>h-soss
por fa-v<u>o</u>r*

Could you give me smaller notes?
¿Podría darme billetes más pequeños?
podr<u>ee</u>-a d<u>a</u>rmeh bee-y<u>e</u>h-tess mass peh-k<u>e</u>n-yoss

Where should I sign?
¿Dónde firmo?
d<u>o</u>ndeh f<u>ee</u>rmo

THINGS YOU'LL SEE

banco	bank
buzón	mailbox
caja	cashier, cash desk
cajero automático	ATM
cambio (de divisas)	foreign exchange
cartas	letters
certificados	registered mail
correo aéreo	airmail
correo terrestre	surface mail
correo urgente	express mail
cuentas corrientes	current accounts
destinatario	addressee
dirección	address
estampilla	stamp

→

extranjero	postage abroad
firma	signature
franqueo	franking
giros	money orders
horas de oficina	opening hours
horas de recogida	collection times
ingresos	deposits
lista de correos	poste restante
localidad	place
paquetes	packages
plata	money
postal	postcard
rellenar	to fill in
remitente	sender
tarifa	charge
timbre	stamp
tipo de cambio	exchange rate
venta de estampillas	stamps
zona postal (Z.P.)	zip code

TELEPHONES

The telephone in Latin America is a source of constant frustration. In the major cities of most countries, you can usually dial direct to the United States and Canada and to some places in Europe. But the situation differs from country to country, and outside the cities telephones are a great deal less reliable. In recent years, the state-owned telephone companies have been privatized, so that in some countries the telephone system is run by several competing companies—complicating matters further. Generally speaking, however, long-distance telephone calls need to be made from the Central Telephone Exchange (**la central telefónica**) where booths are available. These will be marked in different ways: **urbana/ciudad** for local calls; **interurbana/pais/interior** for calls to other places within the country; and **internacional** for international calls. The external area codes vary from country to country, but 09 is often the international code dialed before the code for the country.

The Central Telephone Exchange is usually in the central square of a town, or nearby, and is often known by the name of the telephone company or its initials: **ENCOTEL** (Argentina), **ENTEL** (Bolivia, Peru), **TELECOM** (Colombia), **SETEL** (Ecuador), **CANTV** (Venezuela), **TELCOR** (Nicaragua), **EGT** (Guatemala), **Teléfonos** (Mexico and elsewhere).

Not every country in Latin America has facilities for collect calls abroad. Neither Cuba nor Venezuela has any service at all, while collect calls to Europe are not available, or are very restricted, in El Salvador, Ecuador, Bolivia, and Guatamala. They are difficult to arrange in Paraguay and Uruguay. In Colombia the service is available only from private telephones. Elsewhere (Peru, Honduras, Nicaragua) it is available only from the telephone exchange. In Mexico, by contrast, international calls are so expensive that collect is positively recommended. The service in Chile is generally good, while in Argentina direct dialing for international calls is rarely available.

As well as the Central Telephone Exchange, there are public telephone booths in every country, but they are usually not

very reliable. Most bars and restaurants have telephones for
public use. Most public telephones use coins, although the
rampant inflation of recent years means that the value of the
coins keeps on changing. In Peru, tokens (**fichas**) are used,
obtainable from street vendors and newsstands, while in
Colombia the relevant coins can be bought in batches from the
central post office and telephone exchange.

USEFUL WORDS AND PHRASES

busy	ocupado	*okoopado*
call *(noun)*	una llamada	*yamada*
	(telefónica)	*teh-leh-fonika*
(verb)	llamar (por teléfono)	*yamar por teh-leffono*
cardphone	un teléfono	*teh-leffono deh*
	de tarjeta	*tarHeh-ta*
code	el prefijo	*preh-fee-HO*
collect call	una llamada por	*yamada por kobrar*
	cobrar	
dial	marcar (un número)	*markar oon noomairo*
dial tone	la señal para marcar,	*sen-yal para markar,*
	el tono para marcar	*tono para markar*
direct dialing	discado directo	*deeskado deerekto*
directory	información	*eenformass-yon*
assistance		
extension	extensión,	*ekstenss-yon,*
	anexo *(Arg)*,	*anekso,*
	interno *(Mex)*	*eentairno*
information	información	*eenformass-yon*
international	internacional	*eentairnass-yonal*
operator *(man)*	el operador	*opairador*
(woman)	la operadora	*opairadora*
phone book	la guía telefónica,	*gee-a teleh-fonnika,*
	el directorio	*deerektor-yo*
	(telefónico)	*teleh-fonniko*
phone booth	una cabina telefónica	*kabeena teleh-fonnika*

phonecard	una tarjeta de teléfono	*tarHeh-ta deh teh-leffono*
public telephone	un teléfono público	*teh-leffono poobleeko*
receiver	el aparato	*aparato*
switchboard	la central,	*sentral,*
	el conmutador,	*konmootador,*
	la centralita	*sentraleeta*
telephone	un teléfono	*teh-leffono*
telephone number	el número de teléfono,	*noomairo deh teh-leffono,*
	el fono *(Chi)*	*fono*

Where is the nearest phone booth?
¿Dónde está el teléfono más cercano?
dondeh esta el teh-leffono mass sairkano

Is there a phone book?
¿Hay una guía telefónica?
I oona gee-a teleh-fonnika

Can I call abroad from here?
¿Puedo llamar al extranjero desde aquí?
pweh-do yamar al estran-Hairo desdeh akee

How much is a call to the US?
¿Cuánto cuesta la llamada a Estados Unidos?
kwanto kwesta la yamada a estadoss ooneedoss

I would like to call collect to . . .
Quisiera hacer una llamada por cobrar a . . .
keess-yaira assair oona yamada por kobrar a

Could you give me an outside line, please?
¿Me puede dar línea, por favor?
meh pweh-deh dar leeneh-a por fa-vor

(It's John) speaking
Habla (John)
abla John

Hello (response)

Diga	Bueno (Mex)	Aló (Ven)
d_ee_ga	bw_eh_-no	al_o_

Hola (Col/Per/Arg)	Oigo (Cub)
_o_la	_oy_-go

May I speak to Maria, please?
¿Me comunica con María, por favor?
meh komoon_ee_ka kon mar_ee_-a por fa-v_o_r

Me pasa . . . (Mex)	Me conecta . . . (Arg/Chi)
meh p_a_sa . . .	meh kon_e_kta . . .

Could Mr. Lopez come to the phone?
¿Que atienda/se ponga el teléfono el Sr. López?
keh at-y_e_nda/seh p_o_nga el teh-l_e_ffono el s_e_n-yor l_o_pess

Do you know what time he (she) will be back?
¿No sabe a qué hora regresa?
no s_a_beh a keh _o_ra reh-gr_e_ssa

Extension 345, please?
¿Extensión tres cuatro cinco, por favor?
ekstenss-y_o_n tress kw_a_tro s_ee_nko por fa-v_o_r

Anexo . . . (Arg)	Interno . . . (Mex)
an_e_kso . . .	eent_ai_rno . . .

Will you tell him (her) that David called?
¿Le dice por favor que llamó David?
leh d_ee_sseh por fa-v_o_r keh yam_o_ David

May I leave a message?
¿Puedo dejar recado?
pw_eh_-do deн_a_r rek_a_do

I'll call back later
Volveré a llamar mas tarde
volvair_eh_ a yam_a_r mass t_a_rdeh

Sorry, I've got the wrong number
Disculpe, me he equivocado de número
deeskoolpeh meh eh eekeevokado deh noomairo

You've got the wrong number
Se equivocó de número
seh ekeevoko deh noomairo

I've been cut off
Se (me) cortó la comunicación
seh meh korto la komooneekass-yon

THINGS YOU'LL SEE

América	Latin America
cabina telefónica	phone booth
centralita	switchboard
central telefónica	telephone exchange
ciudad	local
conmutador	switchboard
cospeles	telephone tokens
descolgar el aparato	lift receiver
EEUU	US
ficha	token
fuera de servicio	out of order
guía telefónica	phone book
interior	long-distance
interurbana	long-distance
introducir monedas	insert coins
locutorio telefónico	phone booth
malogrado	out of order
marcar el número	dial the number
monedas	coins
no funciona	out of order
operadora	operator
páginas amarillas	yellow pages

→

país	long-distance
paso (de contador)	unit
prefijo	code
ranura	slot
Reino Unido	UK
reparaciones	complaints department
servicio a través de operadora	dialing through the operator
servicio automático	direct dialing
urbano	local

THINGS YOU'LL HEAR

Diga/Bueno/Aló/Hola/Oigo
Hello

Está llamando
It's ringing

¿Quién habla?
Who's speaking?

¿De parte de quién?
Who shall I say is calling?

No está/No se encuentra
He/she is not in

No cuelgue
Don't hang up

Están comunicando/Está ocupado
The line is busy

¿Con quién desea hablar?
Who would you like to speak to?

¿Mande?
May I help you?/What can I do for you?

EMERGENCIES

Information on local health services can be obtained from
tourist information offices and consulates or embassies. Each
country has its own telephone numbers for fire, ambulance,
and police.

In case of sudden illness or accident, go to the nearest **centro
médico**, **casa de socorro** (emergency first-aid center), or clinic
(**clínica**), or to a hospital emergency room (**urgencias**). If on
the road, look for **un puesto de socorro**, which is also an
emergency first-aid center.

If you are the victim of a robbery or assault, you should
report this to the police as soon as possible. Make sure that the
report is written on the required forms and that it is signed,
sealed, and stamped by the authorities. It is unlikely that your
property will be returned, but the document reporting the theft
will be important, particularly if you have lost identity papers.
Let your embassy know if you have lost your passport.

USEFUL WORDS AND PHRASES

accident	un accidente	*akssee-denteh*
ambulance	una ambulancia	*amboolanss-ya*
assault *(noun)*	asalto	*assalto*
(verb)	asaltar	*assaltar*
break down	tener una pana,	*tenair oona pana,*
	descomponerse	*deskomponair-seh*
breakdown	una pana,	*pana,*
	una descompostura	*deskompostoora*
burglar	un ladrón	*ladron*
burglary	un robo, un atraco	*robo, atrako*
crash *(noun)*	un choque	*chokeh*
(verb)	chocar	*chokar*
emergency	una emergencia	*emair-Henss-ya*
emergency	urgencias	*oor-Henss-yass*
department		
fire	un incendio	*eenssend-yo*

fire department	el servicio de bomberos	*sairveess-yo deh bombaiross*
flood	una inundación	*eenoondass-yon*
hurt	lastimado	*lastee-mado*
injured	herido	*ereedo*
lose	perder	*pairdair*
pickpocket	un carterista	*kartaireesta*
police	la policía	*poleessee-a*
police station	la comisaría	*kommeessaree-a*
rob	robar	*robar*
steal	robar	*robar*
theft	un robo	*robo*
thief	un ladrón	*ladron*
tow	remolcar	*remolkar*
towing service	el servicio de grúa	*sairveess-yo deh groo-a*

Help!
¡Socorro!/¡Auxilio!
sokorro/owkseel-yo

Look out!
¡Cuidado!/¡Abusado! *(Mex)*
kweedado/aboossado

This is an emergency!
¡Es una emergencia!
ess oona emair-Henss-ya

Get an ambulance!
¡Llame una ambulancia!
ya-meh oona amboolanss-ya

Please send an ambulance to . . .
Haga el favor de mandar una ambulancia a . . .
aga el fa-vor deh mandar oona amboolanss-ya a

Please come to . . .
Por favor vengan a . . .
por fa-vor vengan a

My address is . . .
Mi dirección es . . .
mee deerekss-yon ess

We've had a break-in
Nos robaron la casa
noss robaron la kassa

My car's been broken into
Me forzaron el coche
meh forssaron el kotcheh

There's a fire at . . .
Hay incendio en . . .
I eenssend-yo en

Someone's been injured/knocked down
Hay una persona herida/atropellada
I oona pairsona ereeda/atropeh-yada

My car has been stolen
Me robaron el auto/el carro (*Mex*)
meh robaron el owto/el karro

The registration number is . . .
El número de matrícula es el . . .
el noomero deh matreekoola ess el

I've lost my traveler's checks
Se me extraviaron los checks de viajero
seh meh estrav-yaron loss cheh-kess deh vya-Hero

I want to report a stolen credit card
Quiero denunciar el robo de una tarjeta de crédito
kyairo denoonss-yar el robo deh oona tarHeh-ta deh kredeeto

It was stolen from my room
Lo robaron de mi cuarto
lo robaron deh mee kwarto

I lost it in/at . . .
Lo perdí en . . .
lo pairdee en

My baggage is missing
Mi equipaje se ha perdido
mee ekeepa-Heh seh a pairdeedo

Has my baggage turned up yet?
¿Se ha vuelto a encontrar mi equipaje?
seh a vwelto a enkontrar mee ekeepa-Heh

I've had a crash
Choqué
chokeh

I've been mugged
Me asaltaron
meh assaltaron

I've been raped
Me violaron
meh vee-olaron

My son's missing
Mi hijo se ha extraviado
mee ee-Ho seh a estrav-yado

I've locked myself out of my house/room/car
Dejé la llave dentro de la casa/del cuarto/del auto
deh-Heh la ya-veh dentro deh la kassa/del kwarto/del owto

He's drowning
Se está ahogando
seh esta a-ogando

She can't swim
No sabe nadar
no sabeh nadar

Things You'll See

abierto las 24 horas del día	open 24 hours
botiquín	first-aid kit
casa de socorro	emergency first-aid center
comisaría	police station
farmacia de guardia/turno	late-night drugstore
incendio	fire
marque . . .	dial . . .
policía	police
policía de tránsito	traffic police
primeros auxilios	first-aid center
puesto de socorro	first-aid center
servicios de rescate	rescue services
socorrista	lifeguard
taller (mecánico)	garage
urgencias	accident and emergency department

Things You'll Hear

¿Cuál es su dirección?
What's your address?

Sus señas, por favor
Name and address, please

¿Dónde se encuentra usted ahora?
Where are you now?

¿Puede describirlo?
Can you describe it (him)?

¿A qué hora ocurrió?
At what time did it happen?

HEALTH

Most Latin American countries have both public and private health services. Tourists and travelers can normally gain acces to public hospitals (**centro de salud**, **hospital general**, **centro médico**), but there will often be a charge for treatment, and al medicines will have to be bought at a drugstore (**farmacia**, **droguería**), which may be expensive. The standard of facilitie can vary greatly. Cuba is outstanding for the quality of its publi medical care. In addition to public hospitals, there are hospital and clinics in the social security (**seguro social**) system that are normally restricted to members; i.e., those who pay regula contributions from their wages or salaries. Private hospitals ar less crowded, but expensive. You should, therefore, take out adequate medical insurance before you travel to Latin Americ

It is wise to have a medical and dental checkup before travelin and to check with your doctor which inoculations are recomended for the countries you intend to visit. You should carry with you Spanish translations of any refill prescriptions you may need and a translation of a doctor's letter should you suffer from any chronic condition.

Medicines without prescription are extremely common in Latin America; over 50 percent of medicines are sold without prescription across the counter. The traveler should beware, and pay attention to "use by" dates on all medication.

The most common health problems are the effects of heat, cold, and untreated water or milk. Visitors should use bottled or filtered water at all times, and drink only pasteurized milk. In the mountains above 9,800 feet (3,000 meters), altitude sickness (**soroche**) is common, while at sea level in tropical areas insects are probably the greatest danger.

USEFUL WORDS AND PHRASES

ambulance	una ambulancia	*amboolanss-ya*
antibiotics	los antibióticos	*anteebee-yoteekoss*
appendicitis	una apendicitis	*apendeeseeteess*

appendix	el apéndice	*apendeesseh*
aspirin	una aspirina	*aspeereena*
asthma	asma	*asma*
backache	un dolor de espalda	*dolor deh espalda*
bandage	el vendaje	*venda-Heh*
bandage (*adhesive*)	una tirita	*teereeta*
bite (*by dog*)	una mordedura	*mordeh-doora*
(*by insect, snake*)	una picadura	*peekadoora*
bladder	la vejiga	*veh-Heega*
blister	una ampolla	*ampo-ya*
blood	la sangre	*sangreh*
burn	una quemadura	*keh-madoora*
cancer	el cáncer	*kansair*
chest	el pecho	*petcho*
chicken pox	la varicela	*vareeseh-la*
cold	un resfriado	*resfree-ado*
concussion	una conmoción	*konmoss-yon*
constipation	estreñimiento	*estren-yeem-yento*
contact lenses	las lentes de contacto	*lentess deh kontakto*
corn	un callo	*ka-yo*
cough	tos	*toss*
cut	una cortadura	*kortadoora*
dentist	el dentista,	*denteesta,*
	el odontólogo	*odontologo*
diabetes	la diabetes	*dee-abeh-tess*
diarrhea	una diarrea	*dee-arreh-a*
diphtheria	la difteria	*deeftairee-a*
dizzy	mareado	*mareh-ado*
doctor	el médico	*medeeko*
dysentery	la disentería	*deessenteree-a*
earache	un dolor de oídos	*dolor deh o-eedoss*
fever	la fiebre	*fee-eh-breh*
filling	un empaste	*empasteh*
first aid	primeros auxilios	*preemaiross owkzeel-yoss*
flu	la gripe	*greepeh*
fracture	una fractura	*fraktoora*

German measles	la rubeola	*roobeh-ola*
glasses	las gafas, los anteojos	*gafass, anteh-oHoss*
hay fever	la fiebre del heno	*fee-eh-breh del eh-no*
headache	un dolor de cabeza,	*dolor deh kabessa,*
	una jaqueca	*Hakeh-ka*
heart	el corazón	*korasson*
heart attack	un infarto	*eemfarto*
hemorrhage	una hemorragia	*emoraH-ya*
hospital	el hospital	*ospeetal*
ill	enfermo	*emfairmo*
indigestion	una indigestión	*eendee-Hest-yon*
injection	una inyección	*een-yekss-yon*
itch	un picor,	*peekor,*
	un comezón	*komesson*
kidney	el riñón	*reen-yon*
lump	un bulto	*boolto*
malaria	el paludismo	*paloodeesmo*
measles	el sarampión	*saramp-yon*
migraine	una jaqueca	*Hakeh-ka*
motion sickness	mareo	*mareh-o*
mumps	las paperas	*papairass*
nausea	náuseas	*nowseh-ass*
nurse *(female)*	la enfermera	*enfairmaira*
(male)	el enfermero	*enfairmairo*
operation	una operación,	*opairass-yon,*
	una intervención	*eentairvenss-yon*
	quirúrgica	*keeroor-Heeka*
optician	el oculista	*okooleessta*
pain	un dolor	*dolor*
penicillin	la penicilina	*peneesseeleena*
pharmacy	la farmacia	*farmassee-a*
plaster of Paris	la escayola	*eskayola*
pneumonia	una pulmonía	*poolmonee-a*
pregnant	embarazada	*embarrassada*
prescription	una receta	*resseh-ta*
rheumatism	el reúma	*reh-ooma*

scald	una quemadura	*keh-mad<u>oo</u>ra*
scratch	un arañazo	*arran-y<u>a</u>sso*
smallpox	la viruela	*veerw<u>eh</u>-la*
sore throat	un dolor de garganta	*dol<u>o</u>r deh garg<u>a</u>nta*
splinter	una astilla	*ast<u>ee</u>-ya*
sprain	una torcedura	*torsseh-d<u>oo</u>ra*
sting	una picadura	*peeka-d<u>oo</u>ra*
stomach	el estómago	*est<u>o</u>-mago*
sunstroke	la insolación	*eensollass-y<u>o</u>n*
tonsils	las amígdalas	*am<u>ee</u>gdalass*
toothache	un dolor de muelas	*dol<u>o</u>r deh mw<u>eh</u>-lass*
typhoid	la fiebre tifoidea	*fee-<u>eh</u>-breh teefo-eed<u>eh</u>-a*
ulcer	una úlcera	*<u>oo</u>lssaira*
vaccination	la vacunación	*vakoonass-y<u>o</u>n*
vomit	vomitar	*vommeet<u>a</u>r*
whooping cough	la tos ferina	*toss fair<u>ee</u>na*
yellow fever	la fiebre amarilla	*fee-<u>eh</u>-breh amar<u>ee</u>-ya*

I have a pain in my leg
Me duele la pierna
meh dw<u>eh</u>-leh la py<u>ai</u>rna

My eyes hurt
Me duelen los ojos
meh dw<u>eh</u>-len loss <u>o</u>-Hoss

I don't feel well
No me encuentro bien
no meh enkw<u>e</u>ntro byen

I feel faint
Siento que me voy a desmayar
sy<u>e</u>nto keh meh voy a desma-y<u>a</u>r

I have nausea
Tengo náuseas
t<u>e</u>ngo n<u>ow</u>seh-ass

113

It hurts here
Me duele aquí
meh dweh-leh akee

It's a sharp/dull pain
Es un dolor agudo/sordo
ess oon dolor agoodo/sordo

It's sore all the time
Es un dolor constante
ess oon dolor konstanteh

It only hurts now and then
Sólo me duele a ratos
solo meh dweh-leh a ratoss

It hurts when you touch it
Me duele al tocarlo
meh dweh-leh al tokarlo

It stings/It itches
Escuece/Me pica
esskweh-sseh/meh peeka

I have a temperature
Tengo fiebre
tengo fee-eh-breh

I need a prescription for . . .
Necesito una receta para . . .
nesseh-seeto oona resseh-ta para

I normally take . . .
Normalmente tomo . . .
normalmenteh tomo

I have high/low blood pressure
Tengo la presión alta/baja
tengo la press-yon alta/ba-нa

I'm allergic to . . .
Soy alérgico a . . .
soy allair-Heeko a

I have been inoculated against . . .
Me he vacunado contra …
meh eh vakoonado kontra

Have you got anything for …?
¿Tiene usted algo para …?
tyeh-neh oosteh algo para

Do I need a prescription for …?
¿Necesito receta para …?
nesseh-seeto resseh-ta para

I've lost a filling
Se me ha caído un empaste
seh meh a ka-eedo oon empasteh

Will he (she) be all right?
¿Estará bien?
estara byen

How is he (she)?
¿Cómo está?
komo esta

THINGS YOU'LL SEE

casa de socorro	first-aid center
centro de salud	hospital, health center
centro médico	hospital, health center
consulta	doctor's office
droguería	drugstore
farmacia	drugstore
farmacia de guardia/turno	late-night drugstore
ginecólogo	gynecologist

→

115

médico	doctor
médico general	general practitioner
oculista	optician
odontólogo	dentist
otorrinolaringólogo	ear, nose, and throat specialist
pediatra	pediatrician
primeros auxilios	first-aid center
sala de espera	waiting room
urgencias	emergencies

THINGS YOU'LL HEAR

Tome usted ... pastillas cada vez
Take ... pills at a time

Con agua
With water

Mastíquelos
Chew them

Una vez/dos veces/tres veces al día
Once/twice/three times a day

Sólo al acostarse
Only when you go to bed

¿Qué toma normalmente?
What do you normally take?

Debiera de consultar a un médico
I think you should see a doctor

Disculpe, no lo tenemos
I'm sorry, we don't have that

Hace falta una receta médica para eso
For that you need a prescription

CONVERSION TABLES

DISTANCES

A mile is 1.6 km. To convert kilometers to miles, divide the km by 8 and multiply by 5. Convert miles to km by dividing the miles by 5 and multiplying by 8.

miles	0.62	1.24	1.86	2.43	3.11	3.73	4.35	6.21
miles *or* **km**	1	2	3	4	5	6	7	10
km	1.61	3.22	4.83	6.44	8.05	9.66	11.27	16.10

WEIGHTS

The kilogram is equivalent to 2 lb 3 oz. To convert kg to lbs, divide by 5 and multiply by 11. One ounce is about 28 grams, and eight ounces about 227 grams; 1 lb is therefore about 454 grams.

lbs	2.20	4.41	6.61	8.82	11.02	13.23	19.84	22.04
lbs *or* **kg**	1	2	3	4	5	6	9	10
kg	0.45	0.91	1.36	1.81	2.27	2.72	4.08	4.53

TEMPERATURE

To convert Celsius degrees into Fahrenheit, the accurate method is to multiply the C° figure by 1.8 and add 32. Similarly, to convert F° to C°, subtract 32 from the F° figure and divide by 1.8.

C°	-10	0	5	10	20	30	36.9	40	100
F°	14	32	41	50	68	86	98.4	104	212

LIQUIDS

A liter is about 1.75 pints; a gallon is roughly 4.5 liters.

gals	0.22	0.44	1.10	2.20	4.40	6.60	11.00
gals *or* **liters**	1	2	5	10	20	30	50
liters	4.54	9.10	22.73	45.46	90.92	136.40	227.30

TIRE PRESSURES

lb/sq in	18	20	22	24	26	28	30	33
kg/sq cm	1.3	1.4	1.5	1.7	1.8	2.0	2.1	2.3

MINI-DICTIONARY

Where two forms of nouns or pronouns are given in the Spanish, the first is masculine and the second feminine; e.g., "they" ellos/ellas, "this one" éste/ésta.

There are two verbs "to be" in Spanish: ser is generally used to describe people and things (e.g., "he is a doctor" es médico); estar is used to situate things, i.e., answer the question "where?" (e.g., "the station is in the main square" la estación está en la plaza mayor) or to describe a temporary condition (e.g., "he is tired" está cansado). Both forms are given in this order in the dictionary.

a un/una (see page 6)
about: about 16 alrededor de dieciséis
accelerator el acelerador
accident el accidente
accommodations el alojamiento
ache el dolor
adaptor el adaptador
address la dirección
adhesive el pegamento
after . . . después de . . .
aftershave el after-shave
again otra vez
against contra
agency la agencia
AIDS el Sida
air el aire
air-conditioning el aire condicionado
airline la compañía aérea
airplane el avión
airport el aeropuerto
airport shuttle el autobús
  del aeropuerto
aisle el pasillo
alarm clock el despertador
alcohol el alcohol
all todo
  all the streets todas las calles
  that's all eso es todo

alligator el caimán
almost casi
alone solo
already ya
altitude: at high altitude en altura
always siempre
am: I am soy/estoy
Amazon: the Amazon Amazonas
ambulance la ambulancia
America Norteamérica
American (man) el norteamericano
  (woman) la norteamericana
  (adj.) norteamericano
and y; (before word beginning with "i"
  or "hi") e
Andes los Andes, la sierra andina
ankle el tobillo
annoy molestar
another otro
antifreeze el anticongelante
antiseptic el antiséptico
apartment el departamento
aperitif el aperitivo
appetite el apetito
apple la manzana
application form la solicitud
appointment la cita
apricot el albaricoque

are: you are es/está
  (familiar) eres/estás
  we are somos/estamos
  they are son/están
Argentina Argentina
Argentinian *(adj.)* argentino
arm el brazo
arrive llegar
art el arte
art gallery la galería de arte
artist el/la artista
as: as soon as possible lo antes posible
ashtray el cenicero
asleep: he's asleep está dormido
aspirin la aspirina
at: at the post office en Correos
  at night por la noche
  at 3 o'clock a las tres
Atlantic Ocean el Océano Atlántico
ATM el cajero automático
attractive lindo
  (offer) atractivo
aunt la tía
Australia Australia
Australian *(man)* el australiano
  (woman) la australiana
  (adj.) australiano
automatic automático
away: is it far away? ¿está lejos?
  go away! ¡lárguese!
awful horrible
ax el hacha
axle el eje

baby el bebé, el tierno *(CAm)*,
  la guagua *(Chi, Per)*
baby carriage el cochecito
baby carrier el capazo
back *(not front)* la parte de atrás
  (part of body) la espalda
  to come/go back regresar
backpack la mochila

bacon el jamón, el tocino *(Mex)*
  bacon and eggs huevos fritos con
  jamón
bad malo
bag la bolsa
baggage el equipaje
baggage room la consigna
bait el cebo
bake cocer al horno
bakery la panadería
  (selling pastries) la pastelería
balcony el balcón
ball la pelota
banana el plátano, la banana
band *(musicians)* la banda
bandage el vendaje
  (adhesive) la tirita
bangs el flequillo
bank el banco
bar *(drinks)* el bar
  bar of chocolate una tableta de
  chocolate
barbecue la barbacoa
barber's shop la peluquería
  (de hombres)
bargain la ganga
basement el sótano
basket la canasta
bath el baño, la tina *(Mex)*
  (tub) la bañera, la tina
  to take a bath tomar un baño
bathing suit el traje de baño
bathroom el (cuarto de) baño
battery *(car)* la batería
  (flashlight, etc.) la pila
beach la playa
beach ball el balón de playa
beach umbrella la sombrilla
beans los frijoles, los porotos
  (Chi, Arg, Uru)
beard la barba
beautiful hermoso
because porque

bed la cama
bed linen la ropa de cama
bedroom la recámara, el dormitorio
beef la carne de res, la carne de vaca
beer la cerveza, el chop (*Chi*)
before . . . antes de . . .
beginner un/una principiante
behind . . . detrás de . . .
beige beige
below . . . debajo de . . .
belt el cinturón
beside al lado de
best (el) mejor
better mejor
between . . . entre . . .
bicycle la bicicleta
big grande
bill la cuenta
bill (*currency*) el billete de banco
bird el pájaro
birthday el cumpleaños
  happy birthday! ¡felicidades!,
  ¡feliz cumpleaños!
birthday present el regalo de
  cumpleaños
bite (*noun: by dog*) la mordedura
  (*by insect, snake*) la picadura
  (*verb: by dog*) morder
  (*by insect, snake*) picar
bitter amargo
black negro
blackberries las moras
blanket la cobija, la manta, la frazada
  (*Mex, Ven, Chi, CAm*)
bleach (*noun*) la lejía
blind (*cannot see*) ciego
blinds las persianas
blister una ampolla
blizzard la ventisca
block (*in city*) la cuadra
blond (*adj.*) rubio, guero (*Mex*), catire
  (*Cub, Ven, Col*), chele (*CAm*)
blood la sangre

blouse la blusa
blue azul
boat el barco
  (*small*) la barca
body el cuerpo
boil (*water*) hervir
  (*egg, etc.*) cocer
Bolivia Bolivia
Bolivian (*adj.*) boliviano
bolt (*noun: on door*) el candado
  (*verb*) echar el candado
bone el hueso
book (*noun*) el libro
  (*verb*) reservar
bookstore la librería
boot la bota
border el borde
  (*between countries*) la frontera
boring aburrido, pesado
born: I was born in . . . nací en . . .
both: both of them los dos
  both of us los dos
  both . . . and . . .
  tanto . . . como . . .
bottle la botella
bottle opener el destapador
bottom el fondo
  (*part of body*) el trasero
bowl el tazón, la palangana (*Arg, Uru*)
box la caja
box office la taquilla
boy el chico, el joven, el chavo (*Mex*),
  el chaval (*CAm*), el pibe (*Arg*)
boyfriend el novio
bra el sostén
bracelet la pulsera
brake (*noun*) el freno
  (*verb*) frenar
brandy el coñac
Brazil Brasil
Brazilian (*adj.*) brasileño
bread el pan
break (*verb*) romper

breakdown (car) una descompostura, una pana
  I've had a breakdown se me ha descompuesto el auto/el carro (Mex)
breakfast el desayuno
breathe respirar
bribe una coima, una mordida (Mex)
bridge (over river, etc.) el puente
briefcase la cartera
British británico
brochure el folleto
broil la parrilla
broken roto
brooch el broche
brother el hermano
brown (color) café
  (hair, skin) moreno
bruise el moretón
brush (noun: hair) el cepillo del pelo
  (paint) la brocha
  (for cleaning) el cepillo
  (broom) la escoba
  (verb: hair) cepillar el pelo
bucket el cubo, el balde
building el edificio
bumper el parachoques, la defensa (Mex)
burglar el ladrón
burn (noun) la quemadura
  (verb: something) quemar
  (of fire) arder
bus el autobús
  (long-distance) el ómnibus, la góndola (Chi)
  (local) el camión (Mex), la camioneta (Gua), el guagua (Cub), la micro (Chi), la buseta (Col, Ecu)
business el negocio
  it's none of your business no es asunto suyo
bus station la central de autobuses, la terminal de autobuses
busy (occupied) ocupado
  (bar) concurrido

but pero
butcher's la carnicería
butter la mantequilla, la manteca (Arg, Uru)
button el botón
buy comprar
buzzard la águila ratonera
by: by the window junto a la ventana
  by Friday para el viernes
  by myself solo
  written by . . . escrito por . . .
  by bus en autobús

cabbage el repollo
cabinet el armario
cable car el teleférico, el funicular
cactus el cacto
café el café
cake (small) el pastel, el queque (Chi, Per)
  (large) la tarta
  sponge cake el bizcocho, el panqué (Col, Ven)
calculator la calculadora
call: what's it called? ¿cómo se llama?
  (to telephone) llamar por teléfono
camcorder la videocámara
camera la cámara, la máquina (de fotos)
comforter el edredón
camper (vehicle) la caravana, el tráiler
campsite el camping
camshaft el árbol de levas
can (tin) la lata, el bote, el tarro (Chi)
can: can you . . .? ¿puede . . .?
  I can't . . . no puedo . . .
Canada el Canadá
Canadian el/la canadiense
  (adj.) canadiense
canal el canal
candle la vela
candy el dulce
can opener el abrelatas

canyon el cañón
cap (bottle) el tapón
  (hat) la gorra, el gorro
Cape Horn el Cabo de Hornos
car el auto, el automóvil, el carro (Mex)
  (of train) el vagón
carbonated con gas
carburetor el carburador
card (credit card, etc.) la tarjeta
cardigan el cárdigan
careful cuidadoso, cauteloso
  be careful! ¡cuidado!
caretaker el portero, el/la conserje
Caribbean: the Caribbean el Caribe
carpet la alfombra
  (fitted) la moqueta
carrot la zanahoria
cash (verb) cobrar
  in cash en efectivo
  to pay cash pagar al contado
cash machine el cajero automático
cassette el cassette, la cinta
cassette player el cassette
castle el castillo
cat el gato
cathedral la catedral
Catholic (adj.) católico
cauliflower la coliflor
cave la cueva
cemetery el cementerio
center el centro
certificate el certificado
chair la silla
change (noun: money) el suelto, el sencillo
  (verb: money) cambiar
  (clothes) cambiarse
  (trains, etc.) hacer transbordo, hacer
  correspondencia
check (verb) revisar
check (noun: bill) la cuenta
  (money) el cheque
checkbook el libro de cheques,
  la chequera

check-in (desk) la (mesa de) facturación
check in presentarse en la facturación
cheers! (toast) ¡salud!
cheese el queso
cherry la cereza
  black cherry la guinda
chess el adjedrez
chest (part of body) el pecho
  (furniture) el arcón
chewing gum el chicle
chicken el pollo, la gallina
child el niño
  (female) la niña
children los niños
Chile Chile
Chilean (adj.) chileno
chili el ají, el chile (Mex, CAm),
  el locoto (Bol, Per)
china la porcelana
chocolate el chocolate
  box of chocolates una caja de
  bombones
chop (noun: meat) la chuleta
  (verb: cut) cortar
church la iglesia
cigar el puro
cigarette el cigarro
city la ciudad
city center el centro (urbano)
class la clase
classical music la música clásica
clean (adj.) limpio
clear claro
clever listo
clock el reloj
close (near) cerca
  (stuffy) sofocante
  (verb) cerrar
closed cerrado
clothes la ropa
coat el abrigo
coat hanger la percha
cockroach la cucaracha

coconut el coco
coffee el café
coin la moneda
cold *(illness)* un resfriado
  (adj.) frío
  I have a cold estoy resfriado
  I am cold tengo frío
collar el cuello
  (of animal) el collar
collection *(stamps, etc.)* la colección
  (postal) la recogida
Colombia Colombia
Colombian *(adj.)* colombiano
color el color
color film la película en color
comb *(noun)* el peine
  (verb) peinar
come venir
  I come from . . . soy de . . .
  we came last week llegamos la
    semana pasada
  come here! ¡acérquese!
compact disc el disco compacto
compartment el compartimento
complicated complicado
computer la computadora
concert el concierto
conditioner *(hair)* el acondicionador
condoms los preservativos,
  los condones
condor el cóndor
congratulations! ¡felicidades!
consulate el consulado
contact lenses las lentes de contacto
contraceptive el anticonceptivo
cook *(noun)* el cocinero
  (female) la cocinera
  (verb) cocinar
cookie la galleta
cooking utensils los utensilios
  de cocina
cool fresco
cork el corcho

corkscrew el sacacorchos
corner *(of street)* la esquina
  (of room) el rincón
corridor el pasillo
cosmetics los cosméticos
cost *(verb)* costar, valer
  what does it cost?
    ¿cuánto cuesta/vale?
Costa Rica Costa Rica
Costa Rican *(adj.)* costarricense
cotton el algodón
cotton balls el algodón
cough *(noun)* la tos
  (verb) toser
cough drops las pastillas
  para la garganta
country *(state)* el país
  (not town) el campo
cousin el primo
  (female) la prima
crab el cangrejo, la jaiba
cramp el calambre
crayfish las cigalas
cream la crema
credit card la tarjeta de crédito
crocodile el caimán
crowded lleno de gente
cruise el crucero
crutches las muletas
cry *(weep)* llorar
  (shout) gritar
Cuba Cuba
Cuban *(adj.)* cubano
cucumber el pepino
cuff links los gemelos
cup la taza
curtain la cortina
customs la aduana
cut *(noun)* la cortadura
  (verb) cortar

dad papá
damp húmedo
dance (*noun*) el baile
  (*verb*) bailar
dangerous peligroso
dark oscuro
  dark blue azul oscuro
daughter la hija
day el día
dead muerto
deaf sordo
deck chair la tumbona
deck of cards la baraja
deep profundo
delayed demorado, atrasado
deliberately a propósito
dentist el/la dentista
deny negar
deodorant el desodorante
department store los grandes almacenes
departure la salida
departure lounge la sala de pasajeros
desert el desierto
develop (*film*) revelar
diamond el diamante
diaper el pañal
diarrhea la diarrea
diary la agenda
dictionary el diccionario
die morir
diesel, diesel oil el diesel, el gasoil
  (*Ven*), el petróleo (*Arg*)
  (*adj.*) diesel
different distinto
  that's different! ¡eso es otra cosa!
  I'd like a different one quisiera otro
  distinto
difficult difícil
dining car el vagón-restaurante
dining room el comedor
dinner (*evening meal*) la cena
dirty sucio
disabled minusválido

dish towel el paño de cocina
dishwashing liquid el líquido
  lavavajillas
disposable diapers pañales desechables
distributor (*car*) el distribuidor
divorced divorciado
do hacer
  how do you do? ¿cómo le va?
doctor el/la médico
document el documento
dog el perro
doll la muñeca
dollar el dólar
Dominican (*adj.*) dominicano
Dominican Republic República
  Dominicana
donkey el burro
door la puerta
double room el cuarto doble
doughnut la dona
down abajo
  (*downward*) hacia abajo
downstairs abajo
dress el vestido
drink (*noun*) la bebida
  (*verb*) beber, tomar
  would you like a drink?
  ¿quiere tomar algo?
drinking water agua potable
drive (*verb*) manejar
driver el chofer
driver's license carnet de conducir,
  el permiso de conducir,
  el brevete (*Per, Col*)
drugstore la farmacia
drunk borracho
dry seco
during durante
dust rag el trapo del polvo
duty-free libre de impuestos
duty-free shop el duty-free

each *(every)* cada

  300 pesos each trescientos pesos cada uno

ear *(inner)* el oído

  (outer) la oreja

early pronto

earrings los aretes

earthquake el temblor, el terremoto

east el oriente, el este

easy fácil

eat comer

Ecuador Ecuador

Ecuadorian *(adj.)* ecuatoriano

egg el huevo, el blanquillo *(CAm)*

either: either of them cualquiera de los dos

  either . . . or . . .

  o . . . o bien . . .

elastic elástico

elbow el codo

electric eléctrico

electricity la electricidad

elevator el ascensor, el elevador

El Salvador El Salvador

El Salvadorean *(adj.)* salvadoreño

else: something else otra cosa

  someone else otra persona

  somewhere else en otra parte

embarrassing avergonzante, penoso *(Mex)*, violento *(Arg)*

embassy la embajada

embroidery el bordado

emergency la emergencia

emergency brake *(on train)* el freno de emergencia

emergency exit la salida de emergencia

empty vacío

end *(noun)* el final, el fin

  (verb) terminar

engaged *(couple)* comprometido

engine *(car)* el motor

England Inglaterra

English inglés

Englishman el inglés

Englishwoman la inglesa

enlargement la ampliación

enough bastante, suficiente

entertainment las diversiones

entrance la entrada

envelope el sobre

eraser la goma (de borrar)

escalator la escalera mecánica

especially sobre todo

evening la tarde

every cada

  every day todos los días

everyone todos

everything todo

everywhere en todas partes

example el ejemplo

  for example por ejemplo

excellent excelente

excess baggage exceso de equipaje

exchange *(verb)* cambiar

exchange rate el tipo de cambio

excursion la excursión, el paseo

excuse me! *(to get attention)* ¡oiga, por favor!

  (when sneezing, etc.) ¡disculpe!

  excuse me, please *(to get past)* ¿con permiso?

  (questioning) ¿cómo dice?

exit la salida

expensive caro

extension cord el cable alargador

eye el ojo

eyeglasses los anteojos

face la cara

faint *(unclear)* tenue

  (verb) desmayarse

fair *(noun)* la feria

  it's not fair no es justo

false teeth la dentadura postiza

family la familia

fan *(ventilator)* el ventilador
  (handheld) el abanico
  (enthusiast) el fanático
  (football) el hincha
fantastic fantástico
far lejos
  how far is it to . . .? ¿cuánto hay de aquí a . . .?
fare el pasaje
farm *(large)* la hacienda, la estancia *(Arg, Uru)*
  (small) la finca, el rancho *(Mex)*, la chacra *(Arg)*
fashion la moda
fast rápido
fat *(person)* gordo
  (on meat, etc.) la grasa
father el padre
faucet la llave
fax *(noun)* el fax
  (verb: document) enviar por fax
feel *(touch)* tocar
  I feel hot tengo calor
  I feel like . . . me apetece . . .
  I don't feel well no me encuentro bien
felt-tip pen el rotulador
fence la cerca
ferry el ferry
festival la fiesta
fever la fiebre, la calentura
fiancé el prometido
fiancée la prometida
field el campo
fig el higo
filling *(in tooth)* el empaste
  (in sandwich, cake) el relleno
film la película
filter el filtro
filter papers los papeles de filtro
finger el dedo
fire el fuego
  (blaze) el incendio

fire extinguisher el extintor
fireworks los fuegos artificiales
first primero
first aid primeros auxilios
first floor el primer piso
first name el nombre de pila
fish el pez
  (food) el pescado
fishing la pesca
  to go fishing ir a pescar
fish store la pescadería
flag la bandera
flash *(camera)* el flash
flashlight la linterna
flat *(level)* plano
flat tire el pinchazo, la ponchadura *(Mex)*
flavor el sabor
flea la pulga
flight el vuelo
floor el suelo
  (story) el piso
flour la harina
flower la flor
flute la flauta
  (wooden, etc.) la quena
fly *(noun: insect)* la mosca
  (verb: of plane, insect) volar
  (of person) viajar en avión
fog la niebla
folk music la música folklórica
food la comida
food poisoning la intoxicación alimenticia
foot el pie
for: for me para mí
  what for? ¿para qué?
  for a week *(para)* una semana
foreigner el extranjero
  (female) la extranjera
foreign exchange el cambio (de divisas)
forest el bosque
  (tropical) la selva

forget olvidar
fork *(for food)* el tenedor
fortnight la quincena
fourth cuarto
free *(not busy)* libre
  (no charge) gratis
freeway la autopista
freezer el congelador
French francés
French fries las papas fritas
friend el amigo
  (female) la amiga
friendly amable
front: in front of . . .
  delante de . . .
frost la escarcha
fruit la fruta
fruit juice el jugo de frutas
fry freír
frying pan la sartén
full lleno
  I'm full *(up)* estoy lleno
full board pensión completa
funny divertido
  (odd) raro
furniture los muebles

garage *(for repairs)* el taller, el garaje
  (for parking) el garage, la cochera *(Mex)*
garbage la basura
garbage bag la bolsa de basura
garbage can el balde de la basura
garden el jardín
garlic el ajo
gas la gasolina
gas-permeable lenses las lentes de
  contacto semi-rígidas
gas station la gasolinera
gate la puerta
  (at airport) la puerta de embarque
gay gay
gearshift la palanca de velocidades

gel *(for hair)* el gel
German alemán
get *(fetch)* traer
  have you got . . .? ¿tiene . . .?
  to get the train tomar el tren
get back: we get back tomorrow
  mañana estaremos de regreso
  to get something back recobrar algo
get in *(enter)* subirse a
  (arrive) llegar
get off *(bus, etc.)* bajarse
get on *(bus, etc.)* subirse
get out bajarse
  (bring out) sacar
get up *(rise)* levantarse
gift el regalo
gin la ginebra
girl la chica, la joven, la chavala *(CAm)*,
  la chava *(Mex)*, la piba *(Arg)*
girlfriend la novia
give dar
glad contento
glass *(material)* el vidrio
  (tumbler) el vaso
  (wine glass) la copa
glasses los anteojos, las gafas
glossy prints las copias con brillo
gloves los guantes
glue el pegamento
go ir
gold el oro
good bueno
  good! ¡bien!
good-bye adiós, hasta luego
government el gobierno
granddaughter la nieta
grandfather el abuelo
grandmother la abuela
grandparents los abuelos
grandson el nieto
grapes las uvas
grass la hierba
gray gris

Great Britain Gran Bretaña
green verde
grocery store el almacén, la tienda de abarrotes/alimentos, el boliche (*Chi, Arg, Uru*), la pulpería (*Cos, ElS*), la bodega (*Gua, Nic*)
ground cloth la lona impermeable
guarantee (*noun*) la garantía
  (*verb*) garantizar
Guatemala Guatemala
Guatemalan (*adj.*) guatemalteco
guide el/la guía
guidebook la guía turística
guitar la guitarra
gun (*rifle*) el fusil
  (*pistol*) la pistola

hair el pelo, el cabello
haircut el corte de pelo
hairdresser's la peluquería
hair dryer el secador (de pelo)
hair spray la laca
half medio
  half an hour media hora
half board media pensión
ham el jamón
hamburger la hamburguesa
hammer el martillo
hand la mano
handbag el bolso
hand brake el freno de mano
handkerchief el pañuelo
handle (*on door*) el mango
handsome lindo, guapo
hangover la resaca, el crudo, la cruda
happy contento
harbor el puerto
hard duro
  (*difficult*) difícil
hard lenses las lentes de contacto duras
hardware store la ferretería, la tlapalería (*Mex*)

hat el sombrero
  (*woolen*) el gorro
have tener
  I don't have . . . no tengo . . .
  have you got . . .? ¿tiene . . .?
  I have to go tengo que irme
  can I have . . .? ¿me da . . .?
hay fever la fiebre del heno
he él
head la cabeza
headache el dolor de cabeza
hear escuchar
hearing aid el audífono
heart el corazón
heater la estufa
heating la calefacción
heavy pesado
heel el talón
  (*of shoe*) el tacón
hello hola
  (*response: on phone*) diga, bueno (*Mex*), hola (*Arg*), aló (*Ven*)
help (noun) la ayuda
  (*verb*) ayudar
her: it's for her es para ella
  give it to her déselo
  her book su libro
  her shoes sus zapatos
  it's hers es suyo
hi! ¡hola!
high alto
highway la autopista
hill el cerro
him: it's for him es para él
  give it to him déselo
hire alquilar, arrendar
his: his book su libro
  his shoes sus zapatos
  it's his es suyo
history la historia
hobby el pasatiempos
home: at home en casa
Honduran (*adj.*) hondureño

Honduras Honduras
honest honrado
  (sincere) sincero
honey la miel
honeymoon el viaje de novios
hood *(car)* el capó, el capote, el cofre
  (Mex)
horn *(of car)* el claxon
  (of animal) el cuerno
horrible horrible
horse el caballo
hospital el hospital
hot caliente
  (weather) caluroso
  (spicy) picante
hour la hora
house la casa
hovercraft el aerodeslizador
how? ¿cómo?
humid húmedo
hungry: I'm hungry tengo hambre
hurry: I'm in a hurry tengo prisa
hurt: I've hurt myself me lastimé
husband el marido

I yo
ice el hielo
ice cream el helado, el sorbete *(CAm)*
ice pop la paleta
if si
ignition el encendido
ill: I feel ill me siento mal
immediately en seguida, al tiro *(Chi)*
impossible imposible
in en
  in English en inglés
  in the hotel en el hotel
  in Lima en Lima
  he's not in no está
Indian *(noun: Native American)*
  el/la indígena
  (adj.) indígena

inexpensive barato
infection la infección
information la información
injection la inyección
injury la herida
ink la tinta
inn la fonda
inner tube la llanta
insect el insecto
insect repellent
  la loción anti-mosquitos
insomnia el insomnio
instant coffee el café instantáneo
  en polvo
insurance el seguro
interesting interesante
interpret interpretar
interpreter el/la intérprete
interracial mestizo
invitation la invitación
Ireland Irlanda
Irish irlandés
Irishman el irlandés
Irishwoman la irlandesa
iron *(material)* el hierro
  (for clothes) la plancha
  (verb) planchar
is es/está
island la isla
it lo/la
its su

jacket el saco
jam la mermelada
jazz el jazz
jeans los vaqueros
jellyfish la medusa
jewelry store la joyería
job el trabajo
jog *(verb)* hacer footing
joke la broma
  (story) el chiste*

jungle la selva
just *(only)* sólo
  it's just arrived acaba de llegar

kettle el hervidor de agua
key la llave
kidney el riñón
kilo el kilo
kilometer el kilómetro
kitchen la cocina
knee la rodilla
knife el cuchillo
knit hacer punto
knitwear artículos de punto
know saber
  (person, place) conocer
  I don't know no sé

label la etiqueta
lace *(fabric)* el encaje
lady la señora
lagoon la laguna
lake el lago
lamb el cordero
lamp la lámpara
lampshade la pantalla
land *(noun)* la tierra
  (verb) aterrizar
language el idioma
large grande
last *(final)* último
  last week
  la semana pasada
  at last! ¡por fin!
last name el apellido
late: it's getting late
  se está haciendo tarde
  the bus is late
  el autobús se ha demorado
later más tarde
Latin America América

Latin American *(man)*
  el latinoamericano
  (woman) la latinoamericana
  (adj.) americano
laugh reír
laundromat la lavandería automática
laundry *(dirty)* la ropa sucia
  (washed) la colada
laundry detergent el detergente
laxative el laxante
lazy flojo
leaf la hoja
leaflet el folleto
learn aprender
leather el cuero
left *(not right)* izquierdo
  there's nothing left
  no queda nada
leg la pierna
lemon el limón
lemonade la limonada
length el largo
lens la lente
less menos
lesson la clase
letter *(mail)* la carta
  (of alphabet) la letra
lettuce la lechuga
library la biblioteca
license el permiso
license plate la matrícula, la placa,
  la chapa *(Arg)*
life la vida
lift: could you give me a lift? ¿me
  podría llevar en su auto/carro *(Mex)*?
light *(noun)* la luz
  (adj: not heavy) ligero, liviano
  (not dark) claro
light bulb la bombilla, el foco *(Mex)*,
  la lamparita *(Arg)*, el bombillo *(Col)*
light meter el fotómetro
lighter el encendedor
lighter fluid el gas para el encendedor

like: I like it me gusta
  I like swimming me gusta nadar
  it's like . . . es como . . .
  like this one como éste
lime (fruit) la lima
line (of people, etc.) la cola
  to stand in line hacer cola
lip balm la crema labial
lipstick la barra de labios
liqueur el licor
list la lista
liter el litro
litter la basura
little (small) pequeño
  it's a little big es un poco grande
  just a little sólo un poquito
liver el hígado
lizard la lagartija
  (large) el lagarto
lobster la langosta
lollipop el chupete
long largo
lost and found la oficina de objetos
  perdidos
lot: a lot mucho
loud alto
love (noun) el amor
  (verb) querer
  I love Mexico me encanta Mexico
low bajo
luck la suerte
  good luck! ¡suerte!
luggage el equipaje
lunch la comida, el almuerzo

mad loco
magazine la revista
mail (noun) el correo
  (verb) echar al correo
mailbox el buzón
mail carrier (male) el cartero
make hacer

makeup el maquillaje
man el hombre
manager el/la gerente
many: not many no muchos
map el mapa
  a map of Lima un plano de Lima
marble el mármol
margarine la margarina
market el mercado, la feria (Arg, Uru),
  el tianguis (Mex)
married casado
mascara la mascara
match (light) el fósforo, la cerilla
  (sports) el partido
material (cloth) la tela
matter: it doesn't matter no importa
mattress el colchón
maybe quizás
me: it's for me es para mí
  give it to me démelo
meal la comida
mean: what does this mean?
  ¿qué significa esto?
meat la carne
mechanic el mecánico
medicine la medicina
medium-dry (wine) semi-seco
medium-rare (steak) término medio
medium-sized mediano
meeting la reunión
melon el melón
men's room los servicios de hombres
menu la carta
message el recado
Mexican (adj.) mexicano
Mexico México
Mexico City la ciudad de México,
  el Distrito Federal (Mex)
middle: in the middle en el centro
midnight medianoche
milk la leche
mine: it's mine es mío
mineral water el agua mineral

minute el minuto
mirror el espejo
Miss Señorita
mistake el error, la equivocación
mixed-race *(adj.)* mestizo
mom mamá
monastery el monasterio
money el dinero
monkey el mono
month el mes
monument el monumento
moon la luna
moped el ciclomotor
more más
morning la mañana
  in the morning por la mañana
mosaic el mosaico
mosquito el mosquito, el zancudo *(Mex)*
motel el motel
mother la madre
motorboat la motora
motorcycle la moto(cicleta)
mountain la montaña, la sierra
mountain bike la bicicleta de montaña
mountaineering el andinismo
mountain range la sierra,
  la cordillera *(Chi)*
mouse el ratón
mousse *(for hair)* la mousse
moustache el bigote
mouth la boca
move *(verb: something)* mover
  (oneself) moverse
  don't move! ¡no se mueva!
movie la película
movie theater el cine
Mr. Señor
Mrs. Señora
much: much better mucho mejor
  much slower mucho más despacio
mud el lodo
mug el tarro
museum el museo

mushroom el champiñón
music la música
musician el músico
mussels los mejillones, las cholgas *(Chi)*
must: I must . . . tengo que . . .
mustard la mostaza
my: my book mi libro
  my keys mis llaves

nail *(metal)* el clavo
  (finger) la uña
nail clippers el cortauñas
nail file la lima de uñas
nail polish el esmalte de uñas
name el nombre
  what's your name?
  ¿cómo se llama usted?
napkin la servilleta
narrow estrecho
native el/la indígena
  (adj.) indígena
near: near the door junto a la puerta
  near New York cerca de Nueva York
necessary necesario
neck el cuello
necklace el collar
necktie la corbata
need *(verb)* necesitar
  I need . . . necesito . . .
  there's no need no hace falta
needle la aguja
negative *(photo)* el negativo
neither: neither of them ninguno de
  ellos
  neither . . . nor . . . ni . . . ni . . .
nephew el sobrino
never nunca
new nuevo
news las noticias
newspaper el periódico, el diario
newsstand el puesto de periódicos
New Zealand Nueva Zelanda

New Zealander (man) el neozelandés
  (woman) la neozelandesa
  (adj.) neozelandés
next siguiente
  next week la semana que viene
  what next? ¿y ahora qué?
Nicaragua Nicaragua
Nicaraguan (adj.) nicaragüense
nice lindo
  (place) agradable
  (person) simpático
niece la sobrina
night la noche
nightclub el cabaré, la peña
nightgown el camisón
night porter el sereno
no (response) no
  I have no money
  no tengo dinero
nobody nadie
noisy ruidoso
noon mediodía
north el norte
North America América del norte
North American
  (man) el norteamericano
  (woman) la norteamericana
  (adj.) norteamericano
Northern Ireland Irlanda del Norte
nose la nariz
not no
  he's not . . . no es/está . . .
notebook el cuaderno
nothing nada
novel la novela
now ahora
nowhere en ninguna parte
nudist el/la nudista
number el número
nut (fruit) la nuez
  (for bolt) la tuerca

oars los remos
occasionally de vez en cuando
occupied (busy) ocupado
octopus el pulpo
of de
office (place) la oficina
  (room) el despacho
often con frecuencia
oil el aceite
ointment la pomada
OK okay
old viejo
  how old are you?
  ¿cuántos años tiene?
olive la aceituna, la oliva
olive oil el aceite de oliva
omelette la tortilla de huevos
on . . . en . . .
one uno/una
one-way ticket el boleto de ida,
  el pasaje de ida
onion la cebolla
only sólo
open (adj.) abierto
  (verb) abrir
operation la operación, la intervención
  quirúrgica
operator la operadora
opposite: opposite the hotel frente
  al hotel
optician el oculista
or o
orange (fruit) la naranja
  (color) naranja
orange juice el jugo de naranja
orchestra la orquesta
ordinary corriente
other: the other (one) el otro
our nuestro
  it's ours es nuestro
out: he's out no está
outside fuera
oven la estufa, el horno

over . . . *(above)* encima de . . .
    (more than) más de . . .
    when the party is over cuando
        termine la fiesta
    over there por allá
oyster la ostra

Pacific Ocean el Océano Pacífico
pacifier *(for baby)* el chupete
pack el paquete
    (of cigarettes) la cajetilla
    (of candy, chips) la bolsa
package el paquete
padlock el candado
page la página
pain el dolor
paint *(noun)* la pintura
pair el par
pajamas el piyama
palace el palacio
pale pálido
palm tree la palmera
Panama Panamá
Panama Canal el Canal de Panamá
Panamanian *(adj.)* panameño
pancakes los panqueques
panpipes la zampoña
pants los pantalones
pantyhose los pantimedias
paper el papel
    (newspaper) el periódico
paraffin el querosén,
    el queroseno,
    el petróleo para lámpara
Paraguay Paraguay
Paraguayan *(adj.)* paraguayo
parents los padres
park *(noun)* el parque
    (verb) estacionar
parking lights los pilotos, las calaveras
    (Mex)
part *(in hair)* la raya

partner *(spouse, friend: male)* el compañero
    (female) la compañera
party *(celebration)* la fiesta
    (group) el grupo
    (political) el partido
pass *(driving)* rebasar, adelantar
passenger el pasajero
passport el pasaporte
pasta la pasta
path el camino
pay pagar
peach el durazno
peanuts los cacahuetes, los cacahuates,
    el maní
pear la pera
pearl la perla
peas los chícharros, las arvejas *(Arg, Bol,
    Chi, Col)*
peasant el campesino
    (female) la campesina
pedestrian el peatón
peg *(clothes)* la pinza
    (tent) la estaca
pen la pluma
    (disposable) la lapicera
pencil el lápiz
pencil sharpener el sacapuntas
pen pal el amigo por correspondencia
    (female) la amiga por correspondencia
people la gente
pepper la pimienta
    (red, green) el pimiento
per: per night por noche
perfect perfecto
perfume el perfume
perhaps quizás
perm la permanente
Peru Perú
Peruvian *(adj.)* peruano
phone book la guía telefónica
photograph *(noun)* la foto(grafía)
    (verb) fotografiar
photographer el fotógrafo